Seal in the Desert

Moving Past Feeling Stuck

D1091924

HEATHER FRITZ

Safety is everything, and you deserve to feel a peaceful love that grows you, rather than withers away at your very existence. But first, we must find the courage to love ourselves enough to realize exactly what we deserve.

-Heather Fritz

DEDICATION

Teresa, you are the best sister. Thank you for your endless support. God knew I needed you, and you will forever be my favorite Christmas gift.

Dad and Mom, I love you endlessly, and I'm sorry I never shared what I was going through with you.

My friends who always urged me to keep going. Words cannot describe how you have changed the trajectory of my life.

To my extended family: You are one of the biggest reasons why I married him. I will always see you as my family, even if we drift apart. I know this will be hard to read, but the story needs to be told.

RJ, I see you soaring through the valleys as a hawk—released from your depression and at peace. I hope our story helps others.

To Gabby P., I never met you, but since you are no longer here to tell your story, I will tell mine in your honor.

To all of the people who are experiencing emotional abuse and looking for ways to move past feeling stuck, I believe in you. Keep searching for your ocean and never settle.

CONTENTS

ACKNOWLEDGMENTS

To the people who lived in the home in the Mojave desert who kept seals in saltwater swimming pools, your cruelty inspired the title for this book.

To the creators of the Netflix series Maid. Thank you for shining a light on this topic. The impact of mental abuse and words can have on a person are not shared enough. It was not until I found this series that I felt seen. You gave me the courage to call what I experienced abuse. Having items thrown in your direction might make you grateful that the items did not hit you, but someone who loves you would never throw things at you in the first place.

My friend who told me she wished there were bruises and scars, so people would ask. Our words and voices are our scars, and maybe they can help someone else one day, when we share. Thank you for confiding in me and sharing your journey.

My hope is that if you are in an unhealthy relationship, you discover the courage to speak up, and tell your truth.
Seek help.

Domestic hotline abuse number is: 800.799.7233

A NOTE FROM THE AUTHOR

This story doesn't start off happy. I think a lot of our stories aren't always filled with rainbows and butterflies all the time. Sharing these words is the most vulnerable thing I have ever done.

I'm sharing because there is at least one woman that I can think of who is no longer in our world because she was quiet. She did not reach out to others. The signs were there.

I'm sharing because if I had read this, maybe I could have stepped back and left. Hopefully, this memoir can help a friend or loved one. Perhaps, it will give someone you know the self-awareness to never step foot in an unhealthy relationship.

I'm sharing because although it can be very easy for us to smile and pretend like everything is okay on the surface, there are so many people who choose to suffer silently. Some people naturally have such high energy that when they are broken, beaten, and bruised, you can't tell. Some of us prefer to keep our troubles to ourselves, and that is the most dangerous habit. We need to find courage to share what we are going through as this helps us process it.

I'm sharing because, despite all of the darkness, I have found hope. I've chosen to always look for the goodness in others.

Lastly, I'm sharing because although trauma will forever scar us, we can choose to keep living a wholehearted life. We can choose joy and find faith everywhere around us.

On a side note, just because I am choosing to share this, does not mean I am willing to always discuss it.

Please don't look at me with empathetic eyes. If you would like to acknowledge this, please share about my strength, choice to keep going, or that you're grateful I am telling this story.

Please remember to treat others with extra kindness; for we never know the battles that others have endured or are going through.

1 WHO IS HEATHER?

You're probably wondering who the girl behind these words is. Let's take a trip a decade back. If you asked anyone in high school who I was growing up, I'm sure they would share—kind, driven, compassionate, a leader, caring, friendly, willing to listen, and intellectual. I was all of those things in high school but it shifted.

After graduating high school, I discovered I really liked my best guy friend. Of course, it was after summer, and he moved about two and a half hours away for school. We would text all day non-stop and share the silliest little things with each other. I thought it was love. I'm not really sure what it was.

His family didn't approve of this white chick who

barely knew Spanish. They also didn't approve of my weight.

I was always overweight. When I was in sixth grade, kids were into "dissing" each other. It was the cool thing to do, and unfortunately, I would often be the recipient of the insults. The boys teased about how I was so fat. I wasn't extremely large back in the days, but I remember I was larger than the other kids in class. I would try to get skinnier—doing hundreds of sit-ups every night. It never made a difference.

I recall when I was younger, always asking my mom to stop after school for ice cream at Rite Aid. We must have gone at least two or three times a week as a kid. I suppose I never was really taught any self-restraint, and that ended up playing into my lack of self-control as an adult.

Back to the relationship. I wasted a lot of romance in that first relationship after high school. I thought he was the one and gave and gave until I had no more to give. That was the hopeless romantic in me. I always thought love was giving more and more of yourself until you have nothing left. You hope the person you're in

2

a relationship with will reciprocate that love. Most of the time, that didn't happen for me.

We were on different paths, so I broke things off with my high school best friend on April 1st, and clearly it was not a joke. After dating around unsuccessfully, I was invited to a party with my best friend. X Ambassadors has a song called "Skip That Party", and I wish I would have. I was introduced to an older, cute-looking guy who snowboarded. Laughs and liquor later, we exchanged Snapchat handles, and a new romance began.

We would go on fun dates, and he was always so thoughtful. I recall on one of our earlier dates, I met his uncle. His uncle told Ron that I was a keeper, and at the time I was very confused…Were we together? I wasn't sure he never officially asked, so I didn't know. My mind told me I was undeserving of a worthwhile relationship, so I brushed it off. Once again, he never asked…so what did I know? We didn't hold hands or kiss, so how did I know if it was a relationship?

While at the family ranch, he showed me all of the animals. Ron was so compassionate and sweet with the horses. I knew he had a beautiful spirit in his heart from the way he cared for them. If this man can love an animal this much—he surely can love me just as much—despite his bipolar and depression.

After stopping at the ranch, we proceeded to go to Sea World—about a three-hour drive from where we were. It was a long time to talk and listen to music and get to know one another—even more. He told me about his dabbling with drugs when he was younger. He was addicted and was into the rave scene. He said he would be in jail if caught doing some of the business he did. He explained how the demons would mess with his head when he was on ecstasy, and how—at the time—he liked it. It gave him a high that he always wanted more of. He admitted that these drugs created holes in his brain. I just never realized it would be a foreshadowing of his future.

I wish I would have met him during this phase of his life. It would have been an absolute NO. I'm not into this guy. Dating men who were into drugs was always a hard pass for me. But he had done so much healing, and he grew through his experiences. But most importantly he

4

truly got to know God after his drug phase. His yearning for God was what really sold me. I recall there were times when he would give food and money to the homeless. Ron was always trying to help those in need—those less fortunate than him. His Christian actions and the way he treated complete strangers was one of my favorite attributes of his.

When we first met, I convinced Ron how great Mammoth and Big Bear were compared to his usual snowboarding resort—Mountain High. So, we planned a trip to Mammoth. After booking the trip, we realized we should get to know each other and met up for a few different outings. The first three gatherings it rained. I wish I noticed the tears God was sending down, but instead, I was grateful for the water that would give us great snow.

Let's take a moment to get to know Heather at this moment. I was an ambitious, carefree, outgoing lady who thought I could change the world. I was very career-oriented and I loved teaching. I spent three years serving at a title one school as a fifth-grade teacher. I always tried to be a nice, understanding teacher. Some of my favorite projects at school involved starting a coding club, dabbling in animation with my fifth graders, and forming a recycling club with my friend.

No one could put their finger on it, but I was constantly broken down and told I wasn't good enough. Not in my work setting, or from my family, but from my boyfriend at the time. I chose not to tell others. Instead, I wrote notes on my phone. I rarely revisited these notes— as I know they would break me. It was my way of recording the words and shards that I experienced.

When I wrote, I would have the opportunity to know what I experienced was real—that I was not just making things up. Throughout this memoir, I'll be sharing the notes.

I wish I would have shared them with others sooner. There are a lot of things I wish I did differently. For example, if we sought therapy, maybe Ron would still be here. I'm not sure if therapy would have helped a gaslighting narcissist, but I know it helped me.

2 THE FIRST NOTE I FOUND

January 5, 2017
I'm Just Me

I could sit here and cry. Yes. That's easy to do. But reflecting is more challenging. This hurts so much because it's something I've struggled with forever. I don't like being fat. I don't like being judged for being fat. And I'm sorry that the fact that me not being fat is the only thing that could possibly make our relationship better.

Thank you for completely shutting me down. Out of all the people I thought you would understand because at one time you were fat. You taught yourself how to eat healthy (and I think you had support). I could make up a million excuses about all of the time I don't have but the bottom line is I don't have support.

I want support, and I crave support. I don't want to be overweight, unhappy, hidden, and judged anymore.

I'm truly sorry that me being me...just simply isn't enough for you. I wish I was better, and I want to be one day. But an accountability partner or a friend would be helpful and very appreciated.

It's easy to pass judgement, but it's challenging to support someone.

Maybe that's why it is so easy to work with kids. They see me as a person. They see my heart and they see my intentions are good. They understand.

This was written the day before my twenty-fourth birthday. I was sexually denied because I was too fat. Can you imagine being with someone who refuses to have sex with you because they don't accept your size? Neither can I. The most frustrating part about it is he was in the same position at one point. I was hoping he could help me lose weight. But instead, he belittled me. It led to a downward spiral, in which I ate unhealthier and working

8

out was more and more challenging. I am angry I allowed myself to live through this.

We were not living together at this moment, and I should have walked away. I wish I ran away.

If you ever get the urge to walk away, be *bold*, and do it. Move those feet. Run as far and as quickly as you can. You deserve to be happy, no matter your weight, or your value, or if you're poor, or if you have a bankruptcy, or if your past is filled with hundreds of skeletons. Your mental health is not worth staying in a controlling and emotionally abusive relationship. You deserve better. Please learn from my mistakes. Do not let yourself live through this pain.

3 BUYING THE HOUSE

I was commuting two hours a day, and the housing prices near my work were very affordable. So, after I received my Masters in education, I made the jump to buy a home of my own. I was always really motivated and determined to meet goals. However, I never realized the destruction living life as if it was a checklist would cause.

I continued checking off items after receiving my master's degree and purchased a cute four bedroom, three bath house that was about ten years old. It had grass. I knew I would eventually desert-scape it. As grass in the desert is almost as ridiculous as a seal in the desert.

Seal in the Desert

My home was in a little town about twenty miles from Lancaster, called Rosamond. If you've seen Captain Marvel, it's the town where that cool bar was. In fact, I drove by as they were filming that scene, and it was actually a strip club called Zebras previously—I never went. Rosamond also has a military base, an Albertsons, and about three restaurants. It has since expanded though.

At the time, Ron was living in Redondo Beach. So, I told him he could move in with me if he wanted to. He always wanted to buy or move into a tiny home. He was into all the TV shows about downsizing and creating unique tiny homes. I was not completely sold on the idea, so I ended up buying the house.

I used to joke that I bought a home, so that Ron didn't convince us to buy a tiny home. He wasn't on the loan. I bought the house all on my own—as buying a house with someone you've been in a relationship with for less than a year did not seem like a good idea at the moment. He was able to get a job that was closer—so naturally he ended up moving in.

I set yet another checkbox for my made-up checklist of life. I vowed to myself that if Ron did not propose within the next year, he would have to move out. Of course, I never told Ron this. I didn't want to be one of those girls who created unnecessary pressure about the direction I wanted our relationship to grow into.

I was so excited to buy a home at twenty-three. I was the first one of my friends to buy one, and I was looking forward to having people over. Dinners with friends, game and paint nights, but most of all creating good memories with others. I had a handful of get-togethers at the house when I lived there. One get together I can recall was my housewarming party. It was in August, and I had about ten friends over. I looked up a recipe for a delicious sangria mix, and after a few too many drinks—and shots—the night ended with me throwing up. It was a little embarrassing to say the least, but I was not aware of that as I was super wasted.

I wish I invited others to my home more often. It was about an hour and a half from my family which felt too far for friends and family to drive. So, I stopped inviting people over.

I never had a paint night with wine with my friends like I dreamed of. I never invited co-workers over. Ron did not like when I had people over either. He had to be on his best behavior and could not lash out. I can recall a few times when we had another couple over where he would accuse me of flirting with the other guy. It was simply easier to stop inviting people over.

4 THE NEXT NOTE

I'm not sure why it took me so long to write another note.

I know after Ron and I moved in together, it was not easy.

October 26, 2017

Misunderstood

To feel a servant in your own home.

A voice that cannot be heard.

Perhaps I'm not alone.

Feeling guilt for being out late.

Even if it's with work.

Making him wait.

For my presence to be known

Not sure what I'd do wrong tonight.

Seal in the Desert

Anxiously trying to

Avoid another fight.

He could only see the dark in me.

The dark I never thought I had.

And it made me so mad.

I'd be irritated,

Feeling discombobulated.

After being denied sexual pleasure,

He came into the room banging

Pots and pans.

If I can't sleep neither should you,

He thought to himself.

Selfish, he called me.

Inconsiderate.

He came in again.

My body shaking as hell

Wishing to be released from

This evil spell.

I always need to be on the defense

About where I've been.

He doesn't trust me and doesn't care.

The Next Note

If I have things to do

Or things I want to share.

I've talked about myself enough.

Oh, selfish me.

Let me now paint the light

He falls unto thee.

Perfect on the outside.

But a monster within.

Making her gasp for breath as

She's sleeping

Because it's too loud.

Always complaining when

There's something to do.

Even yelling, when I

Accidentally put my shoes

On top of his.

It's all about him.

Dinner tastes bad like this.

Why aren't the dishes done?

What's this on the table?

Seal in the Desert

In this poem, I reflect on how I was accused of cheating on him and all of the toxicity. One night, I came home from grabbing a beer with co-workers. I did not want to have sex, so naturally to him that meant I had engaged in the activity without him.

If you recall in my first note that I shared, I was denied of sex, and I looked inwards. When Ron was denied, he took pots and pans and didn't let me sleep. Then he came back into the room. My body shook uncontrollably, unsure of what might happen next. He would yell, scream, and make me feel so small. He did not hit me, but his words slapped the life out of me.

Perfect on the outside is a perfect description of our relationship. We would go to church together and to a couples class. This was the right thing to do—or so we thought. When we slept together in the same bed, I was told I breathed too loud and it kept him from sleeping. I would try to breathe as quietly as possible, sometimes wishing I would stop breathing.

Yes, there were a few times when I was yelled at for putting my shoes on top of his. It was quite outrageous. The small things would trigger him...so I changed. I had to be so aware of the words I said, the tone I used, the clothes I wore, the things I left laying around in *my* house.

As I mentioned earlier, I stopped inviting people over. I also stopped inviting people in—into my life. I was rarely able to go out with friends or co-workers once we moved in together. Obviously, it was a huge inconvenience when he didn't get a home-cooked meal from his girlfriend. He complained when I cooked that there was not enough flavor, yet he was also upset when I chose not to cook. As a result, I stopped cooking for about four months after Ron left this world. I was terrified he was right. It was easier for me to just have a protein shake if I was able to muster up the courage to consume calories.

He wanted me to ask him permission to go out with friends. So, I started to ask him—not even thinking of the implications. Blinded by his beautiful blue eyes, I did not realize it was extremely unhealthy to ask a partner if I could spend time with friends.

Seal in the Desert

Ron knew that if I could have conversations with other people, I might share about the turmoil I was put through. He wanted me to invite him out too, so he could monitor the conversations. He would talk about himself and his dreams of living in a tiny home. When you're trying to vent about a tough day of teaching to your co-workers and the students that you care for desperately, listening to dreams of living off-grid and composting toilets is not the most appealing.

It got worse. I was told to share my location on my phone. This was just another step in his ploy to control my life and my surrounding world.

I wish he never moved in, and we went our separate ways when I bought the house. He might still be here if he was in a tiny home on his own.

STAYING AFTER I SHOULD HAVE LEFT

You're probably wondering, how did I stay? How was I able to put up with all of this? Why did I choose to? That is a very complex question that I continue to ask myself daily. I have learned from these mistakes and I will never allow myself to even dip one toe into such a toxic place for my being. He had a way of pulling me back in, and when there is sweetness interwoven with the bursts of anger it can be extremely challenging to tell the moments apart.

I will never forget the time we got into an argument, and he ended up throwing the felt letter board. The letter board was changed every so often to Bible verses and sweet love notes. He was upset because there were some items on the front table that did not belong there. After the letters scattered everywhere on the floor, I began crying, and he stomped the board to pieces. I got my phone out to record him, so he could see his anger through my eyes. He noticed that I was recording him. A fire consumed his blue eyes, and he began marching towards me.

Seal in the Desert

He stole my phone out of my hand while
mumbling something like, "You want to record me? Look
what happens." He took it into the garage and smashed it
to pieces.

Stranded in my own home, no phone to
contact family or friends, I sank. In that moment, I knew I
was more stuck than I ever wished to admit.

A few hours later, we made up, but the pieces
of my phone could not be put back together. He said he
would make up for his horrendous act. So, we went to
Costco, and he bought me a new phone. When shown my
phone, the worker asked what happened. We lied and said
my phone was accidentally run over by a car. If I joined his
phone plan, he could get a new phone for free too.

So less than a day after my boyfriend broke my
heart and my iPhone to pieces, I agreed to join his phone
plan because I would get a new iPhone X. Little did I
know, joining his phone plan would be another string that
tied me to him—another opportunity for him to control
me like a puppet. The arguments happened less often and
he continued to grow as a better boyfriend. He eventually

stopped punching walls, breaking things, and began punching pillows instead. I saw the hope in him, and I was very proud of his progress.

We were going to a *very* conservative Baptist church at the time. In our couple's class, we were the only unmarried partners—we were taught about "respect". This was the perfect umbrella and excuse for all of Ron's controlling and manipulating behaviors. Every argument we got in was grounded in the rules of me not respecting him. I respected that man so damn much that I failed to respect myself. If I respected myself, I would have kicked him out of my house.

I felt guilty. I made him change his entire life. I made him change jobs, move in with me, and most importantly—we had two dogs together. What would happen to the dogs? Would he take one—or both—and would they both continue to get beaten? I was also guilt tripped that if I ever left him, he would take his life. He would stop existing because of me. I was not able to walk away because I would be the one who ruined his life.

THE NEXT FEW NOTES

I started to compile a list of the things that Ron did that I needed to talk to him about. I was never able to bring up something he did after he yelled at me or told me I needed to correct something. Most of the time, I never talked about it, so I again wrote notes on my phone.

November 26, 2017

If I bring breakfast in bed, I expect your attention. Don't stay on your phone & ignore me

Followed by "So, we're not having lunch today..." that afternoon.

Can you imagine making breakfast for your significant other, bringing it into the bedroom, and then being ignored? What can be more humiliating than that? Then the *audacity* for the said "significant" other to *expect* you to cook them lunch after they ignored you when you brought breakfast?

This was just a little thing, but there were so many other compiled little events that compounded.

On January 10, 2018, I asked him for the remote, so I could turn off the TV. He ended up throwing the remote angrily on the floor. Was he a man or a man-child? I'm sure at the moment I wanted to chat about something. I understand relaxing is one thing, but throwing a tantrum when you're angry is completely unacceptable.

5 THINGS TO TALK ABOUT

February 2, 2018

I'm disappointed that you don't notice the little ways that I care about you and show my love for you. I know the lease on your car is up, so I let you drive my car over sixty miles each day. This adds up. When I want to sell my car, it's going to have lost value. When I need to get new tires, where does that fall under? If you get a ticket, how does that even work? I let you use my radar detector, and I got a ticket earlier in the year because of that...think about it. When I got my ticket, I didn't blame you for having my radar detector...I just changed my habits.

I make dinner for us almost every night. I treasure the time we have together sitting at the table because I feel like we can look into each other's eyes and talk about our days. But apparently, all I do is talk and talk. So, I'll become aware of that and let you talk more.

When you fall asleep in the other room, I always wake you up for work. I check to make sure you're awake too. Every day, I wake you up for work, and half of the time, I feel like it's my fault you get out of the door late because I didn't wake you up early enough. It puts a lot of extra stress on me.

I feed the dogs almost every morning and every night. I make you breakfast every morning. And I do all of these things without you asking me to.

Yes, these are all simple things, but they take time and energy out of the other things I can be doing.

You made a comment earlier that you do all of the things I ask you to. Yes, you normally do. But should I have to ask you about things like wiping the water off the shower glass door? Or reminding you of the chores that we are splitting? Or cleaning off the dishes then putting away dinner when I've been cooking since I got home?

Seal in the Desert

I feel like whenever you do something, you expect a thank you. I don't get a "thank you" for the simple stupid stuff I do. I don't think I should always have to give one—but I do.

I'm trying to speak to you more respectfully. When you broke my birthday gift, I said in a calm voice, "That is why I don't like the ball being thrown in the house." I didn't say it with an extreme attitude (I thought about it before the words came out of my mouth). I said it calmly. When I asked if you got the glass in the baskets or behind it, you responded with an attitude.

You say that I'm telling little lies about the coffee. First off, I was letting you use my phone while you were pooping! How much more unselfish can I get than that...Then I asked if you wanted coffee. I should've asked louder and been more thoughtful. I'm sorry I wasn't louder about it.

As for grocery shopping, I don't keep a list of the flavors you like in the back of my head. I wish I could pay attention to details for small things like that, and I'll start to pay attention to it. But you gave me a lot of attitude when you said that I didn't get you anything. When

I get an attitude I normally act on the defensive, which I need to work on.

I want you to understand that I'm empathetic. I know that driving two hours to work a day sucks. That's why I am trying to give you a lead for a new job! I don't want you to be unhappy. I don't want you to be stressed. I don't want you to always have shitty days at work.

I want us to work out, too, Ron. And not just the physical work out but both. However, I think we both need to take a step back and realize what we do for each other or maybe what else we can do for each other.

I know I need to start putting you at the same level that I put myself. I'm going to work on it. I also need to work on the way I talk to you.

Please, I want you to be aware that all of my flaws about being selfish, giving attitude, not being organized enough, telling small lies, not buying you the stuff you expect me to buy, not getting you little things to make you happy are destroying me on the inside. They make me feel like I'm not worth it.

How can you love someone else more than yourself if you don't have any self-worth?

Seal in the Desert

I wish I had read it before we got married. My self-worth was diminishing by the moment. I stopped loving myself because I was always trying to put his needs before mine. All of the little digs of not being good enough added up. I wish I could say after time, things got better, but unfortunately, they got worse. A gradual chipping away of my confidence blinded me to what was indeed happening—I was losing myself. There were many reasons I wrote those jumbled words.

Ron ended the lease on his car early, so he could save up to buy me an engagement ring. It was a pretty selfless act. Through it, I let him use my Jetta. At the time, I had the Mazda Miata I was using as my daily car. I eventually ended up selling the Miata to get a Tundra.

Ron was always convinced that if he had a truck, everything would be perfect. They were so useful and practical, and he really wanted one. So, obviously, I started to look for a Tundra for us. I thought that maybe if he had a truck, he would treat me better, and the frustration as well as anger thrown in my direction might diminish. This may come as a surprise, but I thought wrong.

I would often make us dinner, and we were always pretty good about sitting down at the table together, praying, and then eating. There were sometimes where I would talk too much—which I completely agree with. However, the way Ron approached it was always very discouraging. I remember I would always try to plate all of the food with the perfect timing. A few times some of the sides or the food was cold, and Ron chastised me about it. He also hated using the microwave and said it would dry out the food. If I ever criticized his cooking, he would refuse to cook again for weeks at a time, leaving all of the cooking duties to me.

We had a spare bedroom that he would sleep in whenever he was upset. He would also use that bedroom to watch porn and make his girlfriend feel less valued.

To anyone reading these words, I never thought watching porn was a huge deal. But then I saw the way it tore our relationship apart. We aren't created to watch these things. It makes us insensitive and objectifies something that was never created to become just a thing. Also, it sets up unrealistic expectations and creates comparisons for you and your significant other.

Believe me, when Ron would say I wasn't in shape enough, or things to that extent, it broke me. Knowing that he would watch some other person on a screen and then compare my physique to his memories.

He had times where he would watch porn less, and he would ask me to set safety settings on all his devices. But it was always a challenge. I'll never forget the time I spoke up about it, and I said that when he watches porn, I feel like he values me less and thinks less of my body. He replied that the people he watched are a little smaller than me, and if I worked out a little more, it would be better.

I still can't believe I let myself live with, then marry, someone who treated me this way.

I would rise at the crack of dawn to wake up Ron and whenever he was late, that was another burden I took on. I felt like it was my fault that I did not force my grownup boyfriend to get out of bed and out the door at the right time.

I mention that I did a lot of simple things that took time and energy out of the other things I could be doing. Ron always wanted me to work out, but he did not see the little tasks I did that would keep the house moving along. He would help with a lot of the bigger projects, which was always great. I would always try to thank him, but I would not always get "thank yous" in return for the work I did. This was always discouraging.

At the moment, I can't recall what birthday gift was broken, but I do recall I did not like the ball being thrown in the house. Rocket was given her name because she was so fast, and throwing a ball in the house for a fast dog to catch is not the brightest idea.

I would often respond with an attitude or a raised voice. I know I was not the perfect girlfriend or wife by any means. However, I tried to work on it, and when I got an attitude back from him or got yelled at for the simplest things, it was always challenging to respond with love.

Seal in the Desert

I've learned that when we are vulnerable enough to speak our feelings, it is powerful. The way someone responds to our willingness to share is huge. When I would share the deep shards that Ron caused, he often responded with defensiveness. I was shamed for my feelings, and as a result, I became less and less willing to share.

I previously drove a two-hour commute for work, and I was trying to get Ron a lead at a job that was much closer. I had a friend whose husband worked at an aerospace company about twenty minutes away. Ron was able to get hired there.

Sometimes, he was capable of stepping back and seeing the things that I did for him. This was another piece of the complicated puzzle. When I felt seen and appreciated, it was easy for me to forget all of the trials that Ron put me through.

Admittedly, there were times when I did not put Ron first because I was always so laser-focused on my career. He was also just my boyfriend at the time. After we got married, I started to put him before my job, my friends and all of the things I enjoyed.

Isn't that what marriage is? Putting yourself before another person? At what point should you entirely put yourself before someone else? When does it become too much or even toxic to let someone have total control over your life? How did I not recognize these signs? Why didn't I choose to tell anyone about them?

I was too busy painting the perfect life on social media. We had a lot of fun memories and went on countless incredible trips. However, I would let the positive memories overtake any negative feelings I experienced.

As the walls started to close in around me, I began to accept the fate of the swimming pool I lived in as the seal stuck in the desert. Sometimes ignorance is bliss. Unaware of what the world had to offer, I stuck to my cement pool, and I thought it was happiness.

6 THE THREE-MONTH ENGAGEMENT
AND WEDDING PLANNING

It was June 2017. We planned a trip to
Mammoth, but this time we were also visiting family at the
cabin, where I loved going. There is a river that runs
through the backyard, and the way the trees overhang is so
peaceful. Shooting stars can be spotted without any
trouble, and the ambience is simply perfect. Wildlife was
always thriving and walking throughout the land. The fresh
breath of crisp air along with delicious coffee while sitting
among the trees was always one of my favorites.

On our three-hour drive, Ron seemed very
serious and did not want to talk. He was reading or writing

a note and practicing what it said. It was discouraging that he did not want to talk to me while I was driving, but it was okay.

In fact, on our road trips we would get into such horrible arguments over the silliest things that we had systems in place to help prevent them. Of course, these systems disconnected us from one another. Isn't the purpose of a vacation to connect with one another and spend time together? Some examples included using headphones, Ron playing on the Nintendo switch, and me not singing along to songs too loudly. The fact that we disconnected in this way was indeed one of the many things I thought was okay, but it was not.

We stopped at a fish hatchery about twenty minutes from the family cabin, and we walked around. We were looking for cheap places where we could get married. It was pretty but not super romantic.

Ron said he needed to grab something from the car, and I could have *sworn* he was going to propose to me at a fish hatchery. We had never even caught a fish together, so that would have been pretty funny. Luckily, he did not. We got back in the car, and continued our trip to Tom's Place, near Mammoth. I think we were camping in a tent near the river by his aunt's cabin, and it was for two or three nights.

You may have noticed my brain has a hard time remembering a lot of events. It is a trauma response, and one of the main reasons I'm still here. If I let the negative experiences compile, this story might not be written. I taught myself to ignore the challenging times and keep seeking the positive experiences.

On one of the nights while camping, we were surrounded by the campfire with family, and Ron came up to me. He kneeled beside me with a flashlight in his hands, and I got so nervous. My brain raced. Why are you kneeling? Why are you saying my name? Why are you doing this in front of all of these people?

He then said, "Heather, will you go scorpion hunting with me?"

Thank God it was dark outside because I thought he was proposing to me—in front of a majority of his family that I barely knew. Everyone started cracking up laughing. It was admittedly hilarious. But I recall being pretty pissed that night.

Before falling asleep in the tent, Ron asked some questions about what I desired in a proposal. Did I want it to be recorded? Did I want someone else there to take pictures of it? Did I want it to be on a hike? What did I want? I appreciate that he asked for my opinion on these ideas.

The next day, his aunt, Ron, and I hopped in the car, and went on a walk around Convict Lake. We hiked down near the lake, and then Ron said we should stroll down by the water. We got closer, and his aunt stayed back. Then Ron searched in his backpack for something as I looked at the beautiful water.

The edges of the lake were surrounded by beautiful rocks, and Convict Lake had the most stunning turquoise glow to the water which gradually faded into a darker blue. We always loved spending time there.

He pulled a box out of his pocket and proceeded to kneel down. Ron mentioned all sorts of nice things. I realized it was the speech that he was practicing on our drive and the reason he did not want to talk to me.

In the moment, I was so excited and nervous, so I can't recall much of what he said. I said yes, and then we were engaged. Of course, the rugged, manly-man in Ron had to document the moment in nature. He ended up carving our initials and the year into a tree at Convict Lake.

I called a few friends and family members on our way home, and then we immediately began planning. We did the right thing and chose to refrain from having sex until we got married—while we were engaged. Before we were engaged, we were not so morally sound. But we felt as if refraining from the act while engaged would help us grow closer to God and to one another. So, we waited.

A whole three months—the duration of our engagement. We ended up getting wed in August. So many friends and family asked if I was pregnant, and this infuriated me, reminding me of the sexual activity I was *not* having. In retrospect, a three-month engagement was much too short, and we should have waited longer. Maybe if we never started off our relationship fulfilling our sexual desires, I would have noticed the toxic behaviors and how I was being treated so horribly.

The three months we were engaged were stressful to say the least. I found a cheap venue, and I began to piece together what I hoped would be my dream wedding. Did I mention it was stressful? I don't recall having an engagement party. I think we only had a bridal shower because there was such little time between the engagement and the wedding.

Had Ron and I spent more time knowing one another, maybe he would still be on this earth. Maybe we would have realized we were not the most compatible. Maybe I would have chosen to run from the trauma and speak up, saying the way he treated me was unacceptable. Maybe my friends and family would have spoken their doubts and suspicions a little louder.

Seal in the Desert

WEDDING PLANNING

I can vividly recall the stress of planning a wedding in three months. Our first plan of action was to figure out the when and the where. We figured if we could hammer out those details, everything else would fall into place. So, the search began. I was working summer school which was only half days, so the majority of the planning became my responsibility.

If we had less than seventy-five people present, we could have the ceremony at June Lake without a permit and for free. So, we did the most logical thing, and got married there and made sure to have less than seventy-five people. I then proceeded to find a local clubhouse—the Gull Lake Community Center. It was absolutely perfect and very reasonable—less than seven hundred dollars for the venue after the permits and rentals. If you have ever planned a wedding, I'm sure you know this is dirt cheap. There was a moose head on the wall, but it was a fine trade-off considering the convenience, price, and views that overlooked another local lake.

After we had the date and location figured out, it was time to plan a few more details. One of our biggest wedding expenses was our photographer. I posted an ad on Thumbtack, a website to hire freelance photographers. Through the site, we met the most beautiful human. What made him so wonderful? Everything. He had such a beautiful soul and spirit, and his photography is incredible. At the time, his regular price was over three grand. But he cut us a great deal because at the time, I was a teacher. Our gallery is still on his website, if you care to see how happy we looked, and how normal Ron seemed.

It was then time to figure out more details including food, flowers, and a dress…We chose a delicious barbecue place—Copper Top Grill. The catering package was very reasonable definitely less than twenty dollars a person.

I decided I would order flowers from Costco. So, I placed my order with an abundance of baby's breath, sunflowers, and yellow mountain bouquets. I got my dress at David's Bridal. I went on a whim and found the dress the first time I looked. I did not invite all of my bridesmaids to join me or do any of the typical cute wedding things. I didn't have enough time. When God places someone else in my life, and I have the opportunity to get married again, I plan on savoring every moment.

Now the complicated part, when you get wed, you need an officiant. This should not be complicated. However, with the church we were attending, it slowly spiraled into a hot mess. We did not know the main pastor too well, so we asked the leader of our Christian couple's class if he would marry us. He said yes, and we proceeded to think everything was peachy keen. Then the biggest curveball got thrown at us—and mind you, we were planning a wedding in three months, which is a huge challenge in itself.

We met with the pastor at his office one month before our wedding, and he asked us some marriage questions. We, of course, shared that we were being good Christians and refraining from sex while engaged. Are you ready for the curveball? He told us he can travel and marry us, but there will be no alcohol allowed at the wedding.

Yes, you read that correctly. No alcohol allowed at the wedding. Ron was in his very religious stage at the time and honestly considered not having alcohol. Can you imagine going to a wedding that was six hours away and not being able to drink alcohol? I asked if champagne was allowed, and that was also a no. Naturally, we talked it out, prayed about it, and argued for quite some time. Eventually, we came to the consensus that we would have to scramble and find someone else to marry us.

As I was telling my dad all of this drama, he told me there are quick online courses for officiants, and he got to work. Ron and I really wanted a God-loving pastor to marry us. God has always been an important part of my life, and this was non-negotiable for us.

I began calling all ten of the local churches. I finally got on the phone with a pastor from a local calvary chapel church, and he agreed to marry these two crazy adventure-seekers. I think, in a way, we reminded him of himself and his wife. We met with him over video, as well as once before the wedding if I recall correctly.

Seal in the Desert

He had us each take a survey that asked about our lifestyles, and we were supposed to talk about our differences. I remember we took some time to discuss our differences.

My dad ended up getting his online officiant license as well. I loved the way he went through all of that effort to get it—just in case. Our photographer also shared that he was an officiant. However, it might have been weird to have the person taking pictures marry you at the while also documenting such a special day. Would he take a few selfies as we shared our vows?

A photographer, food, flowers, a location, a dress, and an officiant—most of the details were hammered out. Speaking of hammered, we got two kegs of beer from the Mammoth Brewery. We got the Golden Trout Ale and the Double Nut Brown. We also had some wine, and tons of champagne—because of course we were going to do an actual toast. I still cannot believe Ron considered getting married without alcohol. I am very grateful this was an issue that I actually stood my ground on.

I bought and created several different wedding decorations including: the party favors which consisted of tic-tac-toe bags with X and O rocks, small containers that had Mammoth sunflower seeds and dirt. I had no clue Mammoth sunflowers were a thing. It seems they grow a little taller, and rather than having brown in the middle, they have a yellow tone. I even bought my own tablecloths, and mason jar vases.

Then I finally caved and decided it would be the smartest idea to work with the wedding planner who had a student in my class. With the promise of peace-of-mind, it was a no brainer. I remember Ron was upset because he felt it was an unnecessary expense. She was the most down-to-earth wedding planner who gave me an incredible rate and let me use all of her decorations at the last minute. If I ever move out east, I will definitely call her up and have her plan any events I host.

THE BRIDAL PARTY

Obviously, my sister was my maid of honor and she was a complete saint. At only eighteen, she planned a bachelorette party and most of the events that typically occur during an engagement. She would be so stressed, and I always tried to remain calm. She has since vowed to me, if I ever get married again, I need to be engaged for at least one year. I could not agree with her more.

Our bridal party was pretty small. I had three of my best friends and Ron's sister. He invited his best friend, brother, and two of my friends' boyfriends at the time.

Since our wedding was so rushed, we did not have too many get-togethers with the bridal party. Is that even a thing? I truly don't know. I had my bachelorette party with my girls wine tasting in Ojai. It was an incredible experience hanging out with my friends. We spent one night in Ventura and then headed home. Although we had two days together, one night felt a little rushed. I requested no crazy shenanigans as I knew that wouldn't be respectful to Ron. The wildest and most inappropriate part of the celebration was penis confetti—which Ron ended up finding and absolutely berated me about it.

For Ron's bachelor party, he and his guys visited Kernville, went tubing in the river, and enjoyed the hot springs. They drank some hard liquor, which Ron was never great with. He got in a huge fight with my best friend's boyfriend, and it almost ended in a physical altercation.

I've never really talked to the guys who were there about it. However, I'm sure they've put two and two together and have wondered if anything similar ever happened between Ron and I like that.

The fight was over differing social beliefs, and Ron was upset that his friend would not stop talking about his beliefs. This made things very awkward between my best friend and I for a while.

I know she lost a lot of respect for Ron after that, and she did not have much respect for him in the first place. My friend's boo was not able to participate in the wedding party anymore, and originally, Ron didn't even want him at the wedding. However, I stepped in and advocated for myself—one of the very few times throughout our time together—and said he would still be there for our wedding.

ENGAGEMENT PICTURES

Our photographer was phenomenal, and he asked when we could visit Mammoth for engagement pictures. I was concerned as I thought this would cost more money. But he said it was included, and it was a fun way for him to get to know the couple before he documents the biggest day of their life.

Before we met our photographer, we got in a *huge* fight. I don't even recall why, but at that moment, I truly debated calling things off. I wish I would have. Maybe Ron would still be here.

We proceeded to meet the photographer, jumped in his car, and drove to some amazing places to take some really cool pictures. This was the first time in my life when professional pictures were taken—other than school pictures. As you can imagine, it was an awkward situation. Our photographer helped the discomfort by cracking open a beer from Mammoth Brewing company. While exchanging life stories, we sipped on the beer before the shutter began clicking.

Seal in the Desert

Despite the huge fight Ron and I got in just hours before, the photographer truly encapsulated our love for one another. We walked across logs holding hands, made a heart, and explored the beach with each other. In one picture, we went into the water slightly and turn around for a beautiful scene with the Sierra Nevadas in the background, and of course—as Ron always did—he took it one step further. He insisted on being able to flip his hair after wetting it in the lake, and our photographer captured the moment so graciously.

We also took pictures in front of the lake, and the clouds were breathtaking. In one of the photos, there was a bird soaring above us. I never anticipated that bird would be the way I would remember Ron less than three years later.

7 THE BIG DAY AND THE HONEYMOON

Two days before the wedding, I got a small delivery in some boxes from Costco. Upon opening the flowers I ordered, I was very worried. Would there be enough flowers to decorate the aisle, make bouquets, and centerpieces?

My mom and I placed the flowers in three five-gallon buckets filled with water in the spare bedroom with lots of sunlight. After two days, the flowers started to bloom beautifully, and the baby's breath overtook the bucket. The room smelled of sweet, fresh flowers, and reminded me of the garden I always wanted. It was a blissful moment that I still recall to this day.

Seal in the Desert

We loaded up three cars: my Jetta, my dad's car, and the Miata—our honeymoon car. Of course we brought Rocket and Groot—our dogs. They were going to get married at the wedding too- like in *101 Dalmations*. Let's be real, the plan was for them to walk down the aisle. Our incredible photographer suggested that Rocket wear a GoPro on her back, which made for some hilarious footage.

Then it was time. We left the house with our two dogs and began the three-and-a-half hour drive to June Lake. We got gas at our usual stop in Bishop, CA a town along the way. As I was putting gas in the Jetta, I left the door open and was joking around with Ron and my family. Then sneaky Rocket jumped out of the car and almost went on her own adventure at the gas station.

As we made our way into Mammoth, we stopped at the brewery to pick up the two kegs we ordered. They didn't fit in our car, and we ended up asking someone else to fetch them for us.

You might be wondering what flavor our cake was. Well, as you have probably realized by now, Ron and I were never too traditional. We ended up just having a small cake that we bought in Mammoth for ourselves. I remember we were so stressed, and when I went into the grocery store in Mammoth, I called Ron and asked what cake he wanted. He didn't seem to care as there were a ton of other things going on. I bought the cake I thought he would like and showed him, but he ended up yelling at me. I was so selfish for not asking him about the type of cake he wanted at the right time, and I should have known better.

I wish I would have recognized that him not wanting to be a part of the process of choosing the flavor then proceeding to complain I did not involve him and chose the wrong cake was a huge red flag. What are you supposed to do? Call off the wedding the day before, because your fiancé hurts your feelings when you buy the wrong cake?

The rest of the guests got to indulge in a dessert bar filled with cookies, pie, cake cups, and chocolate. Everyone enjoyed a sweet treat on the day that would turn my life sour. I just had no clue at the time.

Seal in the Desert

There was a huge fire in Yosemite for several weeks before our wedding. The national park was just a few mountain ranges over from June Lake, and just a simple shift in the wind could have ruined the fresh air for our wedding. However, it turned out fine. God blessed us with that.

The night before the wedding, Ron's family got the wedding party and our families pizza. We ate while decorating the hall where we were going to have the reception. It was a beautiful time together—and the pizza was absolutely delicious.

While some family was decorating, the bridesmaids and I created flower arrangements together. We also created the bouquets for the tables that night. I was never creative growing up, but the simplicity of putting several different flowers together and making something beautiful made my heart extremely happy. I decided on that day I wanted to work at or own a flower shop in the future. I would love to help other couples or families with their most beautiful or most challenging days with the gift of flowers from God's earth.

The morning of the wedding, I was excited—as anyone would be when you're getting married. Ron delivered coffees for myself and my bridesmaids. My girls gave me a beautiful bracelet to wear on the wedding day and ironically enough, it was the exact same design my mom gave me to wear. Each of my bridesmaids wrote me a sweet note that I read as we were getting ready. One of my friends did my hair, makeup, and helped out with every aspect of the wedding. I truly appreciated her.

After I was ready, our photographer had Ron and I meet in the forest behind our hotel for our first look pictures. We peeked around trees and walked through the forest holding hands. I don't think I let him kiss me. I told him he had to wait until the wedding. I am so grateful for our photographer as he documented the whole day so beautifully.

Following the first look pictures, it was time to drive to June Lake where we would get married on the beach. It looked beautiful. All of our friends and family were waiting for my grand entrance. The bridesmaids made their way in. Then Rocket and Groot came through with Ron's best man. Groot was on a leash. Rocket was prepared for her job to run down the aisle with a GoPro on her back. Obviously, as most dogs do, she had a mind of her own and ran whichever way her heart desired. It made everyone laugh and created an excellent video.

On my dad's arm, I finally got my turn to walk down the aisle. The music didn't play—I suppose that's what happens when I ask a teacher friend to be my DJ. Totally kidding, it turned out absolutely fine, and walking down the aisle to no music was less awkward than I anticipated. I can't recall Ron crying. He always reserved the tears for his manic phases—and today was a happy day.

The ceremony was beautiful with lovely weather. Ron had his vows memorized. I did not. I was too concerned about making sure everything else was perfect, so I read them off a paper.

After the wedding, friends and family offered us words of encouragement and congratulated us. We took a few more pictures with our wedding party, then made our way over to the hall. We had our grand entrance as the new Mr. and Mrs.—wait for it.

I never changed my last name. Ron felt he did not identify with the last name he was given because it was a dad who was never in his life. In our three months of planning a wedding, we decided we would change our names later on and choose the name that meant the most for us. At one point, we even considered combining last names and changing some of the letters around, so I could truly be Mrs. Frizzle—like the Magic School Bus. We ultimately did not make that choice. For our announcement, they announced Ron and Heather.

Then in some other order, we brought out the four-course meal—wait. That's not how it went because we had our favorite BBQ place—Copper Top BBQ in Bishop cater the wedding. The food was delicious, and everyone enjoyed it except one of my friends who had an allergic reaction and, as a result, had to leave early.

We did some of the typical wedding things such as the champagne toast together with our family and friends. We refused to do the money dance. It felt too cringe-y and forced. We also didn't do the garter toss as we felt it was an awkward tradition.

The mother-son and father-daughter dances were a given. Ron always had his way of spicing things up and pulled his aunt onto the dance floor as well. Ron spent a few years after a tougher stage in his life with his aunt and uncle. He always saw them as father and mother figures.

For our dance, my father and I danced to "Daddy's Angel" by T. Carter. We joked the whole time, and I think he might've made me cry a little. He referenced the father-daughter dances we would attend when I was in elementary school and how there were some very interesting themes.

Then it was time for dancing. I spent so much time looking for the perfect music, and songs that were appropriate. Ron and I were very concerned about doing everything that was so honoring to God. In the grand scheme of things, everyone ended up requesting their own songs. It turned out perfect the way it was. I realized that over-planning led to some very stressful details that didn't even matter the day of.

Big Day and Honeymoon

Everyone said our wedding seemed like a big party. I hope when I get married again, that feeling can be recreated. I'll also give myself more time to plan and embrace every moment.

THE HONEYMOON

After spending our wedding night at the Double Eagle Resort and Spa, we had breakfast with my family then made our way through Yosemite to Bass Lake. Some trees were still smoldering as we drove through the national park that decimated Yosemite. At the time, I was too naive to think that our marriage would end in smoke.

We spent the honeymoon in a condo in Bass Lake enjoying each other's company. The condo had a kitchen, and we made delicious breakfast sandwiches before we headed out to explore Bass Lake and Yosemite. One day, we rented a jet ski, and Ron made it his objective to throw me off of it. We got in trouble for going too fast in a reduced-speed area. After avoiding a ticket, we celebrated with the ice cream shop in Bass Lake that has the same ice cream as Disneyland.

One night, we got in a huge argument and wished we did not get wed. I cannot recall the details of the argument, but it was not the conversation one wishes to have with their newly-wed husband—especially on the honeymoon.

Big Day and Honeymoon

In between arguments and being thrown off a jet-ski, we also found time to enjoy a horseback ride through Yosemite. I recall the instructor told me how short my legs were, and it has always stuck with me. We also enjoyed beautiful Yosemite. I don't recall the exact details of yet another argument we got into while driving through the park. However, I do remember contemplating if I made the correct choice. It would have been so easy to just stumble over the edge of one of the beautiful mountains, but I chose not to.

8 THE FIRST MARRIED NOTE

October 5, 2018

When we go somewhere and I actually put on makeup, do you know what I say to myself?

I hope I don't cry this time.
Please think about that.

A year from now (or less) I'll be on anti-depressants, and I'm not going to be the same person. I'll have withered away. All of the light and brightness that comes with my personality is going to be gone.

       Less than two months after we got married, I wrote this note. Throughout our relationship, I stopped wearing makeup. I was not sure when I would be subject to the warm water flowing from my eyes. The car drives were always so stressful. If I sang too loudly or didn't know all of the words, I would be yelled at. I used to love singing, and I think he thought it was a nice attribute of mine. If I was driving and I asked for his attention, I was too much. If he was driving, and I tried to have a conversation, it would typically end poorly.

We would always travel hours away to go to the snow, and it was challenging to say the least. Our drives turned into meaningless distractions because it was easier not to have a conversation. When we were on long road trips, entangled in a fit of words, there were times when I considered just opening the door and being done with the life I was living.

In the note above, I also mentioned being on antidepressants. I was very close to calling the doctor and asking for this medicine. I am not sure if it would numb the pain, or numb my broken heart, but I knew I needed to do something.

I started working at a new school a year after we wed. Not many people noticed my light begin to dim because they did not know me too well. I had one friend who worked at the same school as me previously, and I opened up a little to her. She was one of the only people who I confided in and knew a portion of the struggles I experienced.

I was not really allowed to hang out with friends as they would notice I was different. I was always reserved and refused to tell the people closest to me what I was dealing with.

In this same note, I found some of the reasons I made Ron upset. These included asking him to throw away the trash, when I would wear mint lip gloss, and the fact that we would always have something else going on whenever we visited my parents.

I also found some things I needed to change and work on as a result of our discussion. Some of these things included being more organized, respecting my husband, not following other cars so closely when driving, responding after he berated me, and listening attentively when Ron is excited about something. I was even given some sentences that would help when he was upset including: "I'm sorry that you're upset". As if that was not enough, he also asked me to try to share a positive reinforcement after I say sorry. In my note I jokingly added "and act like a slave".

Whenever we would talk, I always felt unheard. I wasn't able to express my true feelings. Ron suggested that I say, "Can I please say something?" God forbid I try to inteRonect my feelings about something Ron was sharing about and interrupt him.

Instead, I began to shut down more and more. When we would have a "conversation", it was more like a one-sided lecture in which Professor Ron explained all of the things I did wrong. I would try to initiate a conversation, but the blame was constantly turned to me. I stopped talking about how I was feeling because it was just easier.

9 COVID, CAMPING, AND THE SELLING THE HOUSE

In February 2020, Ron and I went on a marriage retreat. We were married for a little longer than a year. I didn't think it was that important, but he really wanted to go, so I chose to go. I cried during almost every lecture. I can't tell you why, but I can tell you I felt horrible. Perhaps I was truly a piece of crap wife. I was always so tired from doing the basics—cooking, shopping, cleaning, and trying to avoid the next shard of words thrown in my direction. In the beginning, I was so motivated. I wanted to be a perfect wife. (Cue Kascey Musgraves song Good Wife). Despite all my tears, we enjoyed the marriage retreat that we attended. I didn't know how to tell Ron that he broke me. After all, this was the man whose words tore me down to the point where wearing makeup was impossible.

A few weeks after the retreat, the world shut down. We were living in the COVID-19 era. It was challenging to find toilet paper, and I wasn't allowed to go into work. Ron envied that I got to work from home. However, he didn't realize work was my escape.

COVID-19 opened my eyes to a lot of things. I loved gardening, and farm fresh eggs from my backyard chickens brought me so much happiness. I took time to breathe. Ron realized he really wasn't happy with his work. He tried to take every waking moment off of work that he could. When he would take time off from work, he would help with projects around the house. We transformed our backyard into a paradise where we could find peace.

We got a third dog. Yes, you read correctly. Two dogs and three chickens were not enough. One day while at Tractor Supply picking up the supplies for our chickens, we saw a flyer for a German shepherd puppy. Obviously, we talked it over in the parking lot for twenty minutes then drove over to the backyard. We met the puppy, and she seemed a little derpy.

As the owners realized we were not interested in her, they showed us another "puppy" they had. A six-month-old mastiff and pitbull mix. Ron walked around, and this dog followed him and looked him in the eyes. This dog was a much better listener. The accidental backyard breeders offered to sell us both dogs for two hundred dollars. We thought about it for a moment then realized doubling the amount of dogs we had would be the stupidest decision ever.

So, we drove home with the mastiff pitbull mix. Naturally, we named him Drax because he was a tough looking dog but nonetheless a sweetheart. All of the dogs are named after Guardians of the Galaxy. I did not post about Drax for awhile on social media as I thought perhaps, we had made a mistake. We got Drax thinking he would solve all our problems. He would keep us entertained during the stay-at-home order and he would help our marriage.

Ron was the harshest on him. He thought that since he was a bigger dog, he had to be tougher. To this day, Drax is still a little apprehensive if you raise your hand a certain way or use a specific voice. I will never ever let someone harm an innocent animal on my watch again.

It was this time during COVID-19 that made me realize we could not have kids. Ron would tell me he did not want to have kids until I lost weight. I was too fat, and growing then raising a child would only make me fatter. I needed to lose weight before we even considered growing our own. He had a really good point. I know this is a struggle that many women experience. However, the delivery of his message was extremely inappropriate.

During COVID, I started working out from home. I would complete Beachbody workouts. It was the first time in a while that I felt confident. I'll never forget sweating, completing workouts, cooking healthier, and hoping for a "Great job, I'm proud of you" from my husband. But instead, Ron told me it was not enough and that I wasn't making good progress.

I could never imagine bringing children into this world with a monster. He was not always a monster, for there were several reasons why I married him. While there were countless memories of joy, and he brought out an adventurous side of me, there were several moments of complete darkness.

The most ironic thing about marrying Ron is that I thought our combined blue eyes would make the most beautiful children. However, it would not be fair to pass the bipolar, depression, and manic genes onto offspring. Ron would get worked up over the smallest things, and raising a child is no easy feat. It is filled with stress and frustration. I knew I would not be able to soothe Ron through his depressive episodes and deal with a child at the same time.

Seal in the Desert

The medicine that he took would make him so grumpy in the mornings. He would fall asleep and, when awoken from his slumber, become enraged. I knew taking care of a child throughout the night would fall solely onto my shoulders, and that was not a responsibility I felt comfortable with. It gave me chills thinking about arguments among Ron and any future children we could potentially have.

He made me feel so worthless, and I would not be able to live with myself if he projected his pain as well as his manic episodes onto our child.

It was so tough to see him deal with Rocket, Groot, and now Drax. Everyone comments on how well-behaved the dogs are, but most people have no clue how they got that way.

As our garden grew during the initial shutdown, I tried to grow into a better person too. We really struggled not being able to go to church, but we tried. I continued working out, and Ron began converting a cargo trailer into a tiny home. He really enjoyed the progress of the project, and we were able to take it on a fun, family trip in July.

CAMPING DURING COVID

July 19, 2020

Lost

I've got no sense of direction,

No idea of discretion.

Got married to a man,

Who breaks me down,

So, I just sit here with my frown.

I can't drink beer because he can't.

I can't go out with friends.

Have to ask permission for everything.

Get monitored daily by the ring.

On summer break but not doing enough,

Shit, this life is tough.

Everything I do ain't good enough,

So, I just sit strong and act tough.

Like none of it bothers me,

But I'm waiting for the perfect moment to flee.

He threatens me with suicide if I leave him.

Says he'll take his life.

But I just want freedom,

Seal in the Desert

Worried about the wreck that I've become.
Don't think I'd ever love anyone.

Wondering why God let me get in this mess,
I'm thinking to myself that it's just a test.

Emotional abuse everyday.
No, I'm not okay.

He's a dog beater,
Joy stealer,
Son of a—wait I like his mom.

Smiling on the outside,
Broken inside,
Thinking everyday of ways to die.

I can't even talk or speak my mind,
Cause then there's another problem that he finds.
The finger always get pointed back at me.
Fuck, I just wanna be free.

Met up with my sister once during a fight.
He turned off my phone, wouldn't let me communicate.
I smile, this life is great.

I get criticized everyday for my weight.
Started working out but it's not okay.
Not good enough,
This life is tough.

Working from home was such a hell.
Wishing there was someone I could tell.

I'm not okay.
I pretend I'm fine.

This poem was written while I wandered into the forest while on a trip in Arizona. I took the dogs with me because it would force me to come back. In this exact moment, I didn't want to exist anymore. This was one of the lowest points I ever experienced. I can't recall exactly how we spiraled into a fight that caused this much pain and destruction on my part, but I knew it was very pent up. I wanted to show him what I wrote and how he made me feel. But instead, I kept it to myself, like I did with most things.

I talk about not being able to drink and go out with friends. He didn't like it if I drank without him. He always said I was able to but would make up excuses for why I should not. He was too tempted to drink, and the doctor told him he couldn't. I was a bad Christian because I chose to drink. The excuses went on and on.

We had Ring cameras at our house,—the backyard, garage, and front door. Just another form of his sick control, Ron would look at them often. He would get mad at me if I came home with coffee. Justifiably, the Starbucks drinks I would enjoy were not healthy and definitely stifled my weight loss progress. The way he knew I drank coffee was from watching the Ring cameras in the garage or at the front door when I walked through. Summer break was my opportunity to rest and rewind, but to Ron, it was my time to put in overtime completing all of the projects around the house.

I always tried to act tough, seeking out the perfect moment to leave. I never found the perfect moment to leave because he would threaten me. I was the glue that held his life together. *But the adhesiveness wore off with every jab, insult, and snarky comment he would throw in my direction.*

I mentioned never wanting to love anyone and questioning why God allowed this. God gave this to me because I could handle it. He filled me with the strength and courage to be able to share this story—to help others through the pain and to never forget my self-worth. I'm so grateful I'm still here to tell you about the challenges and how we can grow through them. When we give it to God, there is nothing He can't help us overcome.

I was so broken, and there were several times that I thought of different ways to die. While on this walk, I thought about just jumping off a rock cliff, and if it would actually remove me from this earth. I'm grateful I didn't because this story needs to be told.

His narcissistic ways would never allow me to speak my mind or share what I was feeling. It would be turned around and I was berated for even daring to feel those emotions, for speaking those words, so I stopped speaking them. I just existed and tried to keep the peace most of the time with the man I was required to spend the rest of my life with.

One time, we got in such a huge fight I ended up driving an hour from where we lived to meet up with my sister.

I called her and said, "I need to get away and meet up." I made it to the mall parking lot where my sister and I were going to meet. We did not have a location yet. Ron called me and told me he was going to kill himself. He then turned off my phone. So, I headed home, worried that my husband's body would be lifeless when I returned.

I was finally able to call my sister, and I told her I was heading home, crying on the phone. She didn't know how bad it was back then. Ron was just the boyfriend-turned-husband who smashed cake in her face when he first met her.

There were two people who I told pieces of the story. My friend and coworker who knew me before it all. She knew about the facade I put on for the world and how I would pretend it was all okay. I also told my best friend, and she knew the pieces of me that would fall apart. She always lent a listening ear.

I ignored the hurt and pain that Ron caused me. Unfortunately, I came to the realization that his bipolar was a piece of him that would break me while simultaneously making me grow stronger.

During July 2020, we spent two weeks in the dense forest near Flagstaff, Arizona. It was our first long trip in the cargo trailer converted tiny home. Not everything functioned perfectly—but we were able to sleep in it for two entire weeks. We enjoyed the bliss it brought about. As a result, the dream of living simpler and in a tiny home began to resurface.

We hung out, played games, and enjoyed our time with several members of Ron's extended family. We took our mountain bikes and rode throughout the forest a few times. All three of the dogs kept us on our feet. Ron beat Drax more times than I can recall while we were on that trip. I begged him to stop, but there was no point fighting with a hurricane.

We ended up visiting the Grand Canyon and it was absolutely breathtaking. We truly enjoyed the views, and my dad joined us. I will never forget my dad's face as Ron got so close to the edge. He looked like he was going to poop himself. Overall, the trip was filled with great memories, despite the walk where I wandered off wallowing in my sadness.

I can't believe I allowed myself to endure the emotional turmoil, but I know I never will again. And surprisingly, I am capable of love and I have since proved it to myself since Ron has chosen to leave this earth.

Seal in the Desert

WORDS LEFT UNSPOKEN

August 30, 2020

I think it would be best we take a break or separate for awhile.

I have no positive feelings towards you—or myself—and I want

to see if it's possible to revive them. I've been the subject of so

many insults and jabs-about my appearance, my lack of wife

duties and common sense, etc. I lack any dignity and self-esteem.

I need to see if it's possible for me to be happy again.

You described me as good-hearted but my heart is turning to

stone, and I want to see if I can preserve the one good quality

that I have. Staying in this relationship is making me question

that God exists. As I endure this pain and begin to rebuild my

faith, I need some time apart.

I'm sorry that I never held up to your physical, emotional, or

mental standards of what you wanted in a woman. I hope in

the future you can find someone that will care about you and fit

your criteria. Please in the future try to fight fair and not bring

up dirty laundry lists.

Covid, Camping, and Selling the House

This was written just days after our two-year wedding anniversary. We spent some time camping in our trailer in Mammoth. I can't remember the antecedent that caused me to write these words, but I recall Ron was upset that I took time out of our vacation to lead a work meeting virtually.

I never spoke these words aloud to Ron, but I found a few notes that had the same underlying message. I was losing myself and crumbling. The man that brought me close to God was the same one whose actions were making me doubt His existence in this moment. My good heart was being thrashed and torn to pieces, but I was not bold enough to share with anyone, so this note sat forgotten in my phone.

At this point, I should have demanded that we attend therapy. I should have found the courage to share my thoughts. But instead, I chose to sit quietly. My light began to dim more and more each day.

Seal in the Desert

THE NEXT NOTE

November 25, 2020

Have you ever been stuck?

Here I sit hiding in my closet, literally upset by the person I've
become. How did I let it get to this?
It's easy to pass judgment, but it's challenging to support someone.

       I never told anyone that I felt stuck—or how
unhappy I truly was. I didn't know who to tell. I did not
know how to admit those words. As a good Christian, I
was always taught that it's important to work things out
between your spouse, and you're not supposed to let the
dirty laundry air out. I see how this is a critical aspect of a
marriage. But when it comes to the point where you are
hiding in your closet to avoid being yelled at for the littlest
thing, it is time to reach out and speak up.

       In retrospect, it's ironic I hid in a closet. I was
the piece of dirty underwear that hugged onto my body. I
knew it was not right to just sit in my filth, but I allowed it
for so long.

       What was I supposed to do, bring all of my
hidden dirt to my friends and family? What would happen
to the dogs? What would happen to me? Ron always said

that he did not want to live without me. He pressured me to stay. He guilted me into prioritizing him and his mental health. As a result, my mental health sank lower than it had ever been.

Maybe a change was exactly what we needed. We decided that it would be a great idea to list our house and move into the cargo trailer that Ron converted. We began this process in November 2020. We decided that at the end of the school year, we would leave California to explore the country and buy a much more affordable property. We would be able to pursue what made our souls happy. Gardening, hunting, raising our own food, and being self-sufficient were ideas that awoke our souls.

We had this hunger to help others see how much value was in life, and how living tiny could bring genuine peace. We dreamed of buying some land and creating a tiny home village—one that had a treehouse, our original cargo trailer build, a skoolie, and a box container house. The idea was that friends and family could visit us, and people who were curious about living a simpler life could have that experience and decide if it was something their hearts truly beat for.

Seal in the Desert

We never made it to that dream. It is so easy for me to sit back and "what if" every circumstance that life has thrown at me. I'm glad that this dream did not work out.

In fact, a friend shared with me that I am lucky he didn't take me too. I don't know if I would be here to write these words if things were slightly different.

SELLING THE HOME

After listing the house in early December, we accepted an offer before we left on our cross-country road trip. Yes, you read that correctly. We took a huge two-week cross-country road trip, instead of packing up our house and down-sizing. I spent the weekends leading up to this trip having garage sales and making a decent amount of money while managing to downsize significantly.

We celebrated Christmas with my family one last time in my house, and then we took off traveling across the country. We took three dogs, our truck, and the tiny home. Other than the flat we got on the side of the freeway, we did not make any scenic stops until we got to Texas where we met up with some friends. The time with them was peaceful, and within a few hours, we were on the road again.

In between driving hundreds of miles, we clung to the hope of checking out some new snowboarding resorts which were a part of the Indy Pass. We really enjoyed snowboarding at Cataloochee Ski Resort in North Carolina. The resort was so accommodating and let us park the truck and trailer right next to their ski patrol. It was perfect for the dogs, which we left in the truck bed.

Seal in the Desert

As we were driving through Nashville,
Tennessee there was an explosion in the city, so we decided
to not go to Ober Gatlinburg and snowboard there.
However, we did buy a few pairs of cowboy boots while
driving through the shops just outside of the resort.

They always get you with the buy two pairs, get
a third pair free. We both bought a pair that had blue
accents in it, and Ron was so excited to send a picture to
his aunt, who basically taught him the value of cowboy
boots and how they are great work boots. The boots I
went with had blue and white flowers on them, and I loved
them. I have not brought myself to wear them yet, but
maybe one day.

West Virginia is where we spent most of our
time throughout the trip, and we visited two resorts—
Winterplace and Canaan Valley. While at one of the ski
resorts, I was recording Ron as he did a trick. I was
apprehensive while standing up on my board and holding
the camera because the hill below me was quite steep. This
resulted in him yelling at me. We were below the ski lift,
and I will never forget someone above yelled, "Don't talk
to her like that."

In that exact moment, I felt such shame, but I also felt seen for the first time in a very long time. If you're given a chance, please be bold and speak up when you hear someone being treated unjustly.

We really loved the snowboarding in West Virginia and scouted a lot of areas where we might possibly be able to relocate while out there. We loved how affordable it was, how kind everyone was, the Andes mint ice cream sandwiches, and the possibility of having a ski resort within an hour from our tiny home village homestead.

One of the cool ideas for our trip was to go from coast to coast, so we started our trip in Ventura Beach, California and traveled to Virginia Beach. We got there by New Year's Eve. Driving underneath the ocean through a huge tunnel was an incredible experience that I will never forget. We also got to walk under the Christmas lights display at Virginia Beach, and it was such a fun experience. At one point, I had our GoPro recording us, and a kid said we were vloggers. We enjoyed a nice dinner and tried blue crab soup, which reminded us of clam chowder.

Seal in the Desert

The road trip continued as we headed to
Virginia to go to yet another snowboarding resort—
Massanutten Resort. The resort had night skiing, so we got
there a little later. By the time we got there, we were
arguing and honestly debating whether we wanted to go
snowboarding. I decided to stay in the truck as Ron put on
his snowboarding gear. This fight was a tough one I can
vaguely recall. He stormed off in his snowboarding gear,
and I stayed with the dogs. He came back about a half
hour later after deciding he did not want to snowboard.
Then we left.

While we were traveling across the country, we
stayed at Walmart parking lots most nights. We used a
website called Freecampsites.net. We were shocked to find
out that Kentucky does not allow parking for longer than
four hours, so we ended up driving through the state very
quickly. The dogs always enjoyed running around at the
rest stops, and it always brought a smile to my face during
the tense times.

Driving across the country is stressful. When I
travel again, I plan on taking my time and focusing more
on the journey rather than the destination. I recall wanting

to stop and look at some caverns as we were traveling, but we felt too rushed to be able to.

We finally made our way back to California after one more flat tire. Colorado, which has the absolute worst roads, surprised us with this flat tire. Reality started to kick in. We were selling the house and moving into this tiny home. This new space was going to be our home.

After returning home, we still had a lot of furniture, outdoor gear, tools, and clothes for two people living in an eight and a half by twenty-foot home. We moved the items into a tent garage Ron set up in the desert near the off-grid property we were planning to move the tiny home to. We moved all of the bunnies, chickens, dogs, excessive amount of Hot Wheels, and our other belongings. Now it was time for the tiny home adventure to begin.

One day it was extremely windy—as it gets in the Mojave Desert. Ron called me frantic because the tent had torn apart from the winds and all of our items were being blown across the desert. The winds must have been thirty miles per hour, and when I arrived at the scene I could not help but laugh. Ron and the man who let us rent the land from him moved all of the items into one of the larger metal storage containers.

I was tasked with taking the pieces of the tent and jamming them into the truck, so we could return it to Costco. I will never forget the comedy I felt when returning a huge ripped tarp up garage to Costco. It was so ginormous it took two carts. I asked a worker to help me roll it in. They returned it without a problem. In retrospect, the canvas garage was not built to be a stand-alone storage shelter. Just as a seal is not meant to swim in the daylight of the desert, confined to such a small swimming pool.

10 TINY HOME LIVING

We left the home in Rosamond in January, 2021, and started living in a tiny home that Ron built himself—out of a Cargo Trailer. Yes, this was the tiny home we stayed in for two weeks while in Arizona and during the cross-country road trip.

It was not the luxurious life that was sold to me when I first learned about tiny homes. In fact, our first night in the tiny home, it rained quite a bit. I woke up in the middle of the night to a wet bed and realized the roof was leaking. In this moment, I truly wondered what I was doing with my life. I just sold the home that I loved. Now I had water leaking on my head and a man that screamed at me lying in my bed. There was not much room for arguments.

Life continued as it normally does, and we found a church that was about forty-five minutes from our off-grid home. We loved the atmosphere there. On Sundays, we would trek out to that little slice of peace. The scenery on the drive to the little church in Green Valley was always breathtaking. After driving past the brown desert, you come around a corner and see grazing livestock among the green grass. It felt like we were in the country filled with the simpler lifestyle that we desired. The first few times we went to church, I would always have tears streaming down my face because the worship music was so beautiful and melodic.

At one point, on our way to church, I choked up the courage to ask Ron if he could please talk to me with that same amount of respect he would show a coworker. He ended up yelling at me for the next twenty minutes on our drive to church. Yet again, I internalized it was not safe for me to share how I was feeling.

Living in a tiny home, I was not allowed to take up physical space, or mental space. A lot happened in that house. I changed. My memory changed. I started to become more obedient because it was easier than trying to speak up and be screamed at.

Although there were challenges, living in a tiny home allowed for more financial freedom. It gave me the opportunity to learn a lot and to appreciate the little things. We used five-gallon water jugs as our water source. As I carried these jugs from where we kept them outdoors about three hundred feet away, to underneath the sink or in the galvanized tub, I would whisper, *"I am a strong, independent woman."*

I am certain that this experience and the words I chanted helped me survive everything I have endured. Find some words that provide you hope and cling to them. Sometimes we need to be our biggest cheerleaders and just keep stumbling forward.

Throughout the rest of this book, I will reference some of my social media posts to describe the healing journey and the memories I forgot.

Seal in the Desert

VALENTINE'S DAY

February 15, 2021

There's no one I'd rather be living tiny (in 156 square feet to be exact) with! Happy Valentine's Day my love! Thank you for everything you do & for the endless beautiful desert sunsets.

You're definitely going to want to tune in to our journey on YouTube at Adventure Awaits with Ron & Heather (link in bio).

This is what I posted on Instagram on Valentine's Day with a picture of us sitting looking off into the distance of the Grand Canyon. Of course, at that time I was too afraid to tell the truth. I walked into work and talked to one of my friends. She looked at me and could tell it was a rough night. I don't think I told her that I had water poured on me while trying to sleep.

Ron would wake up for work in the mornings and leave our tiny home by no later than 4:15 in the morning if he wanted to be to work on time. He had this rule about where we left our shoes, and they had to be off to the side of the walkway. I bent this rule sometimes and would place my shoes carelessly.

On Valentine's Day morning, I woke up to Ron screaming at me at 4:00am because my shoes were in the wrong place. Most wives receive flowers for Valentine's Day, but I was blessed with water dumped on me while I was sleeping.

I wish it stopped there. There is nothing like an arrow to the heart on good ol' Valentine's Day when your husband pours water on you and then begins throwing items in your direction. I started shaking, crying, and hiding underneath the blanket, ashamed that I lived in a tiny metal box, married to someone who would treat me like this. Ron's biggest concern was always respect. He said I wouldn't give him enough respect through my actions. Because of his obvious lack of self-control and respect for me, everything I hoped for on Valentine's Day came crashing down as quickly as the water poured over the bed.

I asked him to please go to work, so I could go back to bed underneath the wet blanket. But things got worse. He started throwing the shoes that were in front of the door towards me. Then he proceeded to take everything on the counters of our tiny home and throw them in the direction of the bed as well.

So, like the good wife I was, I finally got out of bed—shaking and accepting that I would not be able to fall back asleep after this episode. I began cleaning. When I rolled into work, I stopped and got coffee on my way. One of my ways of coping was eating unhealthily or enjoying a calorie-filled mocha after Ron would use me as his punching bag.

Then on February 15th, I posted a sappy picture of us and that there was no one else I would rather be living "tiny" with. What the hell was I thinking? I was spreading these lies to social media, to cover up my complete disgust with myself and the person I had grown into. I suppose social media makes it so easy for us to hide the ugly, vulnerable truth. After all, posting a picture of me crying in bed on Valentine's Day is not something I would have chosen to do while in my survival state of mind.

Although the new owners of the property no longer had seals, it was in this moment that I realized perhaps I was the seal in the desert. I was confined to a metal box and monitored by my location settings. I wasn't allowed to hang out with friends.

The worst part is I knew I was crumbling and did not know who, how, or what to turn to. My skin continued to dry up as my dream of tiny living spiraled into a nightmare of living as a small person—someone who didn't matter.

Seal in the Desert

OFF GRID NOTES

May 2, 2021

Just like the letter board, just like my previous iPhone, just like my car windshield, just like my life.

Shattered.

At this point, I felt hopeless, but I was unsure of where to turn. We were planning on moving across the country in less than two months. Would I remain shattered for the rest of my life?

May 20, 2021
Even shooting stars have their light burn out and turn black.

Shooting stars are not even stars. They are specks of dust or sky trash that falls and burns into the atmosphere creating a burst of light. For such a long time, I was the light that kept both of us trekking onwards, but I was stumbling into a darker and darker place.

May 29, 2021

It has been made clear that we no longer have a future together. I cannot stand this emotional and mental abuse.

As the school year came to a close and our cross-country move to an unknown destination became more imminent, I was fading. I was about to leave behind the things and people that brought me joy—my friends, family, and work. I began to realize how I was being treated was unacceptable, yet again I refrained from sharing these thoughts and words with anyone.

11 CHICKENS, MEMORIES, AND A BUS

After we sold the house, we chose to keep our seven chickens. We loved having fresh eggs. The family we were renting land from also had chickens, so it was always noisy in the mornings, and there were tons of eggs available. When Ron and I started talking about the cross-country move, it was time to start downsizing and thinking about what we could logically bring across the country.

If we had an end destination, it might make sense to bring everything we could and to have challenging living conditions for a few days while traveling. However, with no end destination in mind it didn't make sense to bring seven grown chickens, three dogs, two cars, his motorcycle, and the tiny home across the country without a place to plant our roots.

Since we had so many chickens that were laying, I would occasionally bring the fresh eggs to work. One of my coworkers was really interested in getting some chickens of her own. Naturally, she asked what I would do with my chickens and with the structure we had built for them. I told her she could most likely have them, but I had to check with Ron, and she totally understood.

A few weeks passed, and as Ron and I were driving to visit my family, we were talking about our move. He mentioned that we were going to take all of the chickens with us.

Let's pause for a moment. If you know anything about chickens, you know they are messy and poop a lot and everywhere. It would be unethical for us to keep chickens in a cage for several days traveling across the country. I told him that I told one of my friends at work that she could have some of the chickens, and Ron began to freak out.

We were driving on the freeway, and he started to slam his hands into the dashboard while yelling about how stupid and careless I was. I pulled over and parked the car on the side of the freeway. I was crying hysterically. He was screaming at me, calling me names because I was going to give away all of our chickens and the structure he built for them without asking.

I recall looking in the rear-view mirror, thinking when I might have an opportunity to open my door and walk into oncoming traffic.

Then I realized how unfair that would be for whoever was driving, and whoever would have to live with the fact that they killed someone while driving. Eventually, I drove shakily to the next exit. There was a train station, and he demanded that I park, so he could get out of the car. I was so worried that he was going to walk in front of the train, and I was going to lose him forever.

As the sun began to set, and it got cold, he eventually called me and asked me to pick him up. I cannot recall if the car ride home was extremely silent or if it was filled with apologies. In fact, there are several details from all of the fights that we have had that I cannot remember. My brain has this way of blocking out the pain, and I think that was my way of surviving the marriage. After all, I did not have many options.

THANKS FOR THE MEMORIES

There were undoubtedly lots of good times with Ron. Some of my favorite memories while we were living off grid included the sunsets and our Costco runs together when we would try to convince one another how we did not need every cool outdoor thing that Costco had to offer.

June Mountain and Mammoth Mountain were our favorite places to snowboard, and we always enjoyed our time on the hill shredding the gnar. There were a variety of different ways we stayed overnight at these resorts. Sometimes we rented a hotel room, other times camping in the back of the camper shell while another time we camped in a tent that was in the back of the truck. Nothing compared to getting the first powder runs after a fresh bit of snow. Ron challenged me to be the best snowboarder I could be, and it was a hobby we enjoyed together.

As usual, we were getting into a new hobby— rock climbing. There was an indoor gym in Valencia, local to where my family lived. Ron was always great about pushing me, and rock climbing was no exception. After buying our own harnesses, chalk bags, and rock climbing shoes, we decided to up the ante and purchase outdoor climbing gear.

We went down to the REI Garage Sale in hopes to find a good deal on used rock-climbing gear. On our way down to the REI Garage Sale, we got into a fight because I checked my email and got the presentation that showcased me as Teacher of the Year. Ron was infuriated that I would bring up work—even a great achievement when we were on a date. We were sitting in traffic when this happened.

After withstanding Los Angeles traffic and being screamed at, we found out that rock climbing gear cannot be resold because it might be defective. Originally, I told Ron that our budget should be no more than two hundred dollars. He ended up spending an exorbitant amount. We never had the opportunity to use the ropes, backpack, and other rock-climbing supplies he purchased.

A good memory I can recall involves one of our last day trips together. We trekked up to the Kern River and I got a really cute Boomerang of Ron being adventurous on some rocks in the river. We got coffee, and I think we were singing on the drive up. The beginning of the ride was a little rocky as Ron had gotten in a huge argument with his best friend.

I begged Ron to stop texting his friend and to pay attention to his wife. He finally stopped texting, and I remember how nice it was to have his attention. However, I was on damage control at this point, trying to soothe his disappointment from the argument he got into.

Another fun memory was when we visited Vasquez Rocks, and we hiked around for a little. After all of Ron's expertise in rock climbing, he decided he was going to free climb a little. He ended up landing incorrectly and twisting his ankle. I drove as fast as I could to get to the gas station, so we could get ice. As a result of his injury, he took off several weeks from work and had to be in a boot. This undisputedly resulted in the further decline of his mental health.

Seal in the Desert

THE BUS

It was finally summer. I could feel the freedom on my lips and the beginning of a new journey. We were finally ready to set sail and discover the plans God would reveal to us on the road. I just finished up my teaching job, and we went to the end of the school year party together. Ron hung out with some of the guys but felt a little uncomfortable because he was not drinking.

He always enjoyed hijacking the conversation and told several of my friend's husbands about our tiny living.

During March and April, we spent countless hours looking up buses for sale at auctions, and determining what the best bus would be. We had our off-grid tiny home, but we knew a bus would give us more light and would hopefully be a little cooler. We checked Facebook marketplace quite often.

The night of the party, I showed Ron two different partially converted school buses located in Arizona. One bus was just eight hours away with the other bus an additional two hours away. So, we made plans to visit both of them on Sunday, June 6.

We left very early in the morning, and we attended church in Lake Havasu. Ironically, the man selling a nine-window blue bus was a pastor. He bought it to convert with plans for his family to live in. After driving it across the country to transport his items, he realized it was too small. The pastor did a lot of the tough work already. He took off all of the signs, removed the seats, and painted the bus. The bus was a beautiful blue color, and he just put on new tires and replaced the batteries. It was the same color as my Bible, and we thought it was a sign. However, the bus had over three hundred thousand miles.

Ron and I talked about it, pulled money out of our checking account, but ultimately chose to drive an additional two more hours to Apache Junction, Arizona where we looked at another bus. The second bus was more built out and was gutted but had some rust on the bottom of it.

After driving it around for a little while, an engine light came on which was worrisome. There were several skull decorations in the bus, and Ron always hated skulls as they reminded him of the devil. We sat, talked, and debated on which bus we were going to drive home with.

We even called the pastor—the man with the blue bus in Lake Havasu and debated with him. He was able to knock down the price for us, and we parted ways from the silver, rust bucket in Apache. The pastor met us on our way, and we signed paperwork at a gas station. It was already dark as we made our drive home.

I had no clue how much slower our long drive would be with a bus that had a top speed of fifty-five miles per hour, and my husband, who was driving the bus for the first time. We ended up making a few stops off the road to wake up and stretch our legs. We were rushing back to our off-grid tiny home and back to the dogs.

When we were about an hour and a half away, I told Ron I could no longer drive, and that we needed to pull off. We took some time, and I slept on a very uncomfortable bench in the bus while freezing cold. After a few hours of sleep, I was ready to continue our trek back to the off-grid property. We got back as the sun was rising, and it made for a beautiful picture. Ron stood with his boot—due to his sprained ankle—with Rocket next to him, looking off towards the distance with the bus.

When we got home, we found a chicken the dogs had attacked. Originally, I walked outside and thought why is there a toupee hair piece on the floor? Ron ended up beating the dogs, and he beat Drax so hard that he was unable to walk properly on one leg for a long time. It pained me to think the man who I might have kids with one day could do this to our dog. In that moment, I vowed to never have kids with him. It was the final straw.

We got home very early on Monday morning, and this caused Ron to take his medicine exactly when we got home—almost twelve hours later than usual.

11 THE DAY THAT FOREVER CHANGED ME

June 8, 2021

This was the worst day of my life. I woke up and went to the courthouse to deal with the "red light" ticket I got. Back in May, I got pulled over for going through a yellow light. The officer stated that since I ran the light right in front of him, it was basically just asking for him to give me a ticket.

At the time, Ron and I were planning on moving across the country, so I would not be able to fight the ticket if we were planning on traveling. In the moment, the officer was so disrespectful. When he walked up to my car, he had his hand on his gun holster which was terrifying. Flustered, I could not find all of my documents.

He mentioned I was lucky that I was only getting a ticket for running the red light.

Anyway, this cop wrote the wrong address, and it took the Kern County Sheriffs over two months to input the information into the system. I drove to the courthouse, hoping to get more information or at least give my updated address before we embarked on what should have been the next chapter of our lives. Upon arrival at the courthouse, they told me I had to call a phone number. I drove back home to our off-grid tiny home.

What could have made June 8th the worst day of my life—other than the court house debacle? I just finished up my job with school, and we were officially free. Ron was still confined to his hobbling twisted ankle and his boot which held his pained foot in place. But overall, the new chapter was about to unfold. We drove home a beautiful blue school bus that we intended on building into a tiny home. We were going to complete the simplest of conversions before we hit the road.

On June 8th, we had dentist appointments scheduled for both of us. Ron did not have the best dental hygiene, but was not what made June 8th the worst day.

Seal in the Desert

Ron's first project involved taking out the horrible air seat that the bus had. We did not have an air seat replacement in mind, but he was planning on switching it with one of the sprinter chairs that we got when we purchased the bus. Ron told me that I needed to be ready to help him, at every moment throughout the day and he also mentioned that he felt like he was going to lose it.

I'm not sure if I've mentioned this before, but I was *never* really a helpful person—in his eyes at least. I never knew exactly what he wanted. I tried to work on communication with him, but whenever we tackled a new project, it was always so stressful.

There are so many moments that occurred on June 8th that I wish I could rewrite. But I can't. So, I'll write them here, and maybe I'll find peace in the pieces I'm choosing to share.

When Ron mentioned he was going to lose it, I should have stopped him for the day. We should have rested and relaxed, rather than trying to push through. I went back into our tiny home as Ron was working in the bus, and I started to call the courthouse to get things situated with the stupid yellow light ticket I received. I waited on hold, and in the moment, Ron was yelling for me to help him. I didn't hear him. But then I heard a *bang*. He had thrown something against our trailer to get my attention. I had no idea that this would not be the only time or reason that I called the sheriff department on that day.

I finished up the phone call, and the fire started to *rage* in his eyes. He went into a full-on manic moment. I was supposed to be there for him, and I wasn't. I was simultaneously trying to edit footage for a stupid YouTube video about the exciting new bus we bought. But this was not the help Ron wanted or needed.

When he started to yell, I grabbed the keys to my sedan. While walking past him, he grabbed my shoulders, shook me, and yelled at me. I can't remember the words he said because I was in such shock. I was disappointed that I was planning on leaving this life behind and traveling with someone who shattered me.

But I was stuck and drowning in muck deeper than I cared to admit. It was too late to stop the plans we had laid out. As I got in my car, Ron picked up a rock and threw it at the door. The mark is still there, and it haunts me to this day. He went to our makeshift gate that we used to keep the dogs in our area of the property, and he threw it down and motioned for me to leave.

I chose to stay. I always chose to stay, and perhaps that's what broke me the most.

I ran into the tiny home after Ron and more arguing erupted. In rage, which is an emotion I *rarely* allow myself to experience, I knocked over a bucket that had the GoPro and a few other things that were very unimportant.

Ron then took it a step further, and took the peat moss bucket, which is something we kept in the bathroom to *literally* cover our shit, in the composting toilet. He threw it onto the floor, and it spilled everywhere.

He screamed, *"Do you even care about me?"*.

Up until this moment, I like to think of myself as Ron's lifesaver. *I was always trying to be his flotation device, like a buoy. But every fight, every jab, every insult, broke me. It gradually chipped away at my buoyancy. I did not have the endurance to keep allowing his words to silently break me.*

So, I finally said something back. I yelled back, "When you act like this no."

Then he pushed past me and grabbed it.

As he pushed past me again, I tried to stop him. This time, he forcefully pushed me down to the floor. I tried to stop him from closing the stupid custom rolling barn door that I loved so much. I never realized it would bring me such destruction and despair.

He yelled at me to "go away", and that's the last I ever heard from my husband.

A loud bang emerged. Life stopped for one of us, and it was changed forever for the other. I screamed.

Fairy tales never mention the lover who screams at them in rage or pours water over their partner while they're trying to sleep on Valentine's Day. Happily-ever-afters never talk about the turmoil that you experience in love. Is that even a part of love? I know that when you have two imperfect people, things won't always be ideal. However, I never anticipated this.

I didn't know what to do. I never really got service in the tiny home—after all it was a metal box. I ran outside to call 911 on my cellphone. The woman I spoke to on the phone told me to check if there was a pulse and asked me more details. I broke through the stupid fucking barn door. There was no pulse.

Seal in the Desert

Just his lifeless body, leaning up against the stupid galvanized metal tub I was so adamant on having in the tiny home bathroom. Sometimes they're used as planters in places, and despite the beauty growing inside of the planter, seeing these in public reminds me of his lifeless body.

The lady on the 911 call asked me to lean his body over and perform CPR. I've taken CPR and first aid classes several times throughout my life, but nothing could have ever prepared me for this. The trauma of hearing what ended my husband's life, the visuals I saw, and the smell of gunpowder. My heart will forever go out to firefighters, EMTs, doctors, police officers, and anyone who chooses to see those horrid scenes of lifeless bodies.

I couldn't lift his body. I was too weak. I promised myself—maybe not in that exact moment to never be that weak or incapable again.

The dispatcher asked me for my address. I didn't know where I lived. I couldn't think of the street name or the address. As I was trying to do CPR and move the lifeless body of my husband, she was trying to ping my location.

Day That Forever Changed Me

After the failed attempt at CPR, I had to run down the dirt driveway and search for the ambulance, fire truck, and sheriffs. I stayed on the phone with the dispatcher from 911. She told me to go to the nearest cross streets. The three dogs followed me and ran in different directions. I yelled at them while simultaneously crying my eyes out. I almost threw up and was very dehydrated. The dispatcher reminded me to stay calm, to take deep breaths, and encouraged me to stop my endless wailing. She didn't want me to faint.

I stopped caring about the dogs at that moment. They did not have collars on; I know very irresponsible of us. I saw the ambulance going down the wrong street, several hundred feet away from me. Trying to get their attention, I began to flutter my hands in the air while running towards the vehicle. I was very out-of-shape at this point in my life, and the only running I engaged in was letting the episodes on TV run on. I told the dispatcher that I found the ambulance, and she talked to the paramedics for a moment. Then they invited me into the ambulance.

After I got in, Rocket magically appeared. They let her ride in the ambulance with us. She stayed close to me the whole time. At that moment, I realized that's exactly why dogs are a man's best friend—or in my case a woman's best friend. She did not leave my side on the hardest day of my life and magically found me when I needed her the most.

The sheriff's cars arrived. I think there were two. Everything gets muddled from here. I think there might have been a fire truck too, but I don't completely recall. It took a few hours for the coroner to arrive. I don't remember if the paramedics entered without the sheriffs or how everything happened.

I recall several people telling me it wasn't my fault and that I needed to promise I wouldn't blame myself. The people who owned the house and the land we lived on helped with the dogs, and she gave me the biggest hug, reminding me that it wasn't my fault. I felt so comforted in her arms. The sheriff asked me if I wanted a chaplain to come. I said absolutely.

I don't recall if I was questioned when the chaplain arrived, but I remember being asked details about Ron's suicide. I told the sheriff we were fighting. I don't recall telling him that Ron pushed me. He asked if Ron ever threatened to kill himself before. I was ashamed by my answer. It was yes. But Ron always told me that if I called the police, it would make everything worse. I asked him to go to therapy or counseling, but he wouldn't. I could have pushed harder or followed up.

To my recollection, a half hour later, the chaplain came. He was so comforting and reminded me that since Ron knew God, he was out of pain and was in a better place. He prayed with me and shared that this wasn't my fault. If I didn't hear it so much on that first day, I probably would not have believed it. Sometimes, I still have a hard time believing it.

Then it was time to say goodbye. I'll never forget the paramedics or maybe the sheriffs who carried the remains of my husband on a gurney. The chaplain and I walked over and said a quick prayer. I tried to reach for his hand, calculating exactly where it might be, buried underneath the blue body bag, and I squeezed it.

I always felt like I needed to be strong. I never told anyone the words Ron said that broke me. I grew into a bitter soulless robot that listened to his every word. In fact, when I thought about how I would tell my family, I thought I would just drive myself there. I kept playing a scene of me showing up to my dad's workplace, with the

three dogs behind me in the Jetta. And telling him that
Ron was gone—that he took his life.

The chaplain asked me to call someone, so they
could meet me as I was in no place to drive, and I probably
would not be for several days. I tried calling my dad. He
didn't answer. I called my mom. She didn't answer either.
Then I called my sister—the one who helped plan the
wedding in three months. And she answered. I found the
courage to mumble the words that Ron was gone—no
longer on this earth. She left work immediately and got my
dad.

They arrived to the off-grid property within an
hour and a half. When my dad and sister arrived, we stood
in a circle and hugged for what felt like forever. The three
of us, in that circle, holding onto one another, helped give
me some life in my barren, depleted heart. My mom ended
up driving separately and arrived about twenty minutes
later.

The chaplain stayed with me until my family
was able to drive me "home" or back to their house. We
were told that the sheriffs would contact his family and let
them know of the devastating loss of his mom's first-born
son. We thought there was going to be a sheriff sent to

their house to deliver the news. I called the coroner or the deputy several times the next day and did not hear back. After what felt like forever, we found out that there would not be a sheriff to deliver the news, but that we would need to. So, I tried calling, and texting, and it took a while to hear back.

Finally, my dad broke the news to his dad. It was heartbreaking to hear. They were in such shock. I still don't know if they knew I was present when it happened. If they're reading this, and this is how they find out. I am sorry, and I love you. I wish I had control, but I lost it.

12 THE UPSIDE DOWN

I will never forget how cold I felt on the drive
to my new home—the home where I lived with my family
before I bought my house. We never really enjoyed living
there. It is not a home but rather a building with walls and
a roof. But slowly, it became a place the dogs and I got
more accustomed to. The difference this time was there
was another person in the equation—my grandma. This
woman chose not to be a part of our life for the past ten
years, and like the good Fritz family does, we welcomed
her in.

My sister was so gracious and allowed me to
stay in her room with the dogs as I began to figure things

out. The first few weeks, Rocket and Groot would hop the fence in the backyard and escape. I imagine they were looking for their dad. Ron was always a good lover of dogs —when he wasn't too strict on them. He gave them so many cuddles and taught me that a dog is more of a family member than just an animal. We would bring the dogs everywhere with us. Whenever we would visit his parents, they always looked forward to seeing their grand-puppies.

My summer plans swiftly shifted from traveling the country and finding a place to plant our roots—to moving back in with my parents—at almost thirty and making arrangements to bury my dead husband. I began figuring out what this new displaced life would consist of. I found serenity in the little lake down the street.

The water brought back so many memories. The experience of no worries when I rented kayaks and taught stand up paddle board lessons. The times when life was so much simpler. I would spend my weekends joking and hanging out with the kayaking crew. I even had the opportunity to teach underprivileged youth how to camp and use a propane stove.

It was complete bliss to have my toes in the water again and to paddle board my way to peace. I got bold and began bringing Rocket. Most of the time, she would sit calmly on the front of the board. I felt like one of those gondola rowers from Venice, towing along my incredible dog who would no longer need to worry about being beaten. We were free, but with freedom came new responsibilities.

I struggled with eating and lost fifteen pounds within the first month after losing Ron. It felt good losing the weight, and I was getting a lot of compliments about my new appearance. I made the jump to join the gym. I figured this would be the perfect way for me to gain an appetite back, while toning up, and also shedding pounds in a healthy way.

I grew obsessed with the gym, and I am so grateful that it was my main way of coping with my anger, frustration, disappointment, and trauma. Admittedly, there were quite a few times when I would go to the gym, just so I could go grab a beer from a local brewery afterwards. I figured it was a good way to balance my emotions. Also working out and drinking beer would inherently force me to eat some food.

Although I did not talk, and still don't talk to many people at the gym, it became a sort of sanctuary for me. A place where I knew I could push myself to be my best. It was a start over, a place where people didn't look at me with empathetic eyes but rather a place where I could truly let loose. I began boxing, imagining that each punch was me kicking the gun out from underneath his chin. I don't know what would have happened if I had the courage or strength to do that. But I had promised that I would never allow myself to feel so weak or helpless again, and this was a promise I followed through on.

The songs I box to have made me tougher. I boxed to songs like "Shots" by Imagine Dragons and songs by Papa Roach with lyrics that rang so true. Whenever working out and stumbling upon a song that talks about suicide, it gets added to my boxing playlist. One of my favorite songs that I found strength in was "My Own Monster" by X Ambassadors. Whenever my gloves hit the bag, the monster was released, and I felt a little better. In that moment, I grew into a tougher version of myself, one that would kick butt if someone ever tried to break me down again or physically assault me.

The summer of 2021 was very upside down for me. The absolute opposite of everything I anticipated it would be. But I discovered myself again. I found the

Seal in the Desert

Heather that was buried so deep inside, the version of me
I wasn't allowed to be. I did not need to hide my
personality, censor what I said, or walk on eggshells
anymore.

THERAPY

My best friend is a therapist. She joined my parents and I on June 9th, when we went to the off-grid property and tried to gather up the belongings. After seeing what was left of the scene, my friend knew I would need a lot of support. She convinced me I needed to go to therapy, and I cannot thank her enough for this. In the moment, I was under the impression that she could be my therapist, which is the main reason why I signed up. I called my doctor's office, and I knew exactly what to ask for.

Luckily, my best friend's therapy company accepted my insurance. This sped up the entire process, and I was in my first virtual session within two weeks after losing Ron. I opted to get support through virtual therapy because this was the most convenient option for me. Originally, I was not sure about this decision. But when I was able to hang out with my friends and walk away for an hour for my virtual therapy session, it was very freeing.

Therapy has a very misconstrued reputation. In fact, one night I overheard a loved one say that, "only crazy people go to therapy." I think everyone can benefit from therapy. But as with most things in life, you only get what you put into it. If you stay closed off and don't share what you're truly going through, it will not benefit you. Since it was against ethics, my best friend could not be my therapist, so I was assigned another kind woman. She was a Christian and such a light. She tied a lot of the lessons I learned into Christ's love for me, and she truly helped me to process the things I went through.

When someone listens, uninterrupted, and tells you that you did not deserve that, there is something so freeing. It was so nice to let all of the secrets loose. To tell someone I was having trouble eating, and that I hated my body image. To tell someone basically everything I have opened up on these pages about.

There is something so liberating about sharing our hardships with others. I have had so many unexpected people reach out to me and tell me they have experienced verbal and emotional abuse as well. My hope is that if you are reading this, you have the courage to speak up and seek the help you need. Or help a loved one who might be silently sitting in the shadows hoping no one notices how they are being broken down and avoiding the conversation.

Perhaps you're reading this, and you are debating whether therapy will be beneficial to you. I say go for it.

Without therapy, I would be a whole different person. In fact, I doubt I would be telling this story. Perhaps I would have grown cold and decided to turn my back on the world. I recall at the end of one of my virtual sessions, while at the beach, my therapist told me I needed to listen to "Take Another Step" by Steve Curtis Chapman. The lyrics that struck me the most involved being paralyzed but choosing to take another step. I chose to keep taking steps forward.

Therapy has changed my life and my perspective on everything. We are blessed with the moments we have on this earth, and it is so important to take each one in for what it is. To be mindful of the presence we leave in this world. To be cognizant of our words and of the energy we put into this universe.

FINDING PEACE AT THE BEACH

I spent the first month after losing Ron watching sunsets at the beach and feeling the water on my skin. I recalled that just a few weeks earlier, my mom, sister, Ron, and I were at the beach—celebrating my mom's birthday. I thought it was going to be one of the last times I hung out with my mom and sister. After all, the plan was to leave the state.

I never anticipated I would be back in my hometown—enjoying the sunsets at the same beach, but without him. I never thought the goodbye I would say would be to Ron. I always knew he struggled with depression, bipolar, and suicidal thoughts, but I never imagined he would act on those feelings.

Back to the memory at the beach, I recall Ron hated sunscreen. When I put it on his back, he did a squirmish dance that reminded me of a child when being forced to eat peas in a jar. He was hobbling around still. I know his sprained ankle was a big component to his decline in mental health. He brought a deck of cards for us to play. The cards featured survival tips, and we had fun giggling as we were playing games just sitting on the beach.

Ron must not have gone to the beach too often when he was younger because he decided it would be a good idea to feed a seagull. Can you imagine, this man, sitting on the beach, with a boot on his foot, due to his sprained ankle, being attacked by seagulls, because he chose to feed one seagull a French fry? The seagull carried the entire box of French fries away. Ron was not able to chase the vile bird because of his ankle and I missed it. I think I was floating in the ocean, taking in what I thought would be my last time touching the California coast—for a while at least.

But the biggest coincidence, or as I like to call it, Godwink happened after Ron passed when I found myself back at the beach with my sister and our friend. We were relaxing, and I looked up to see a tall man in the distance, holding the hand of a boy and walking on the beach.

I knew in my heart that it was my friend, but I was so curious as to why my friend, who lived almost three hours away, was at a beach so far from home and why exactly on this day. I told my friends and began running off to meet up with him. The girls must have thought I was delusional—and rightfully so. I had lost my husband, was barely sleeping or eating, and I got drunk off of two beers. While running after my friend, I was trying not to be obvious in case it was not him. This friend is very tall, so it took me about five minutes to finally catch up with him and his son.

When I walked up, I said his name, and his son's name. His son gave me a kiss, which he doesn't give to just anyone. I knew that was a sign from God. This friend asked, "Where is Ron?" and I immediately started bawling my eyes out. At this time, I had not publicly announced that Ron was gone yet. I had kept the news to a very small group of people. I needed to announce it when I was ready and in my timing.

My friend—who was from church—told me that his wife was sleeping in the hotel room. We decided it would be a great idea to surprise her. We knocked on the door, I saw her, and I gave her the longest hug. I didn't want to let go. This friend has the biggest heart, and she is on fire for God. Everything she does shows God's grace. We worked together at a school, and she was always so empathetic. I have never met someone with a bigger passion for helping others. She asked me what was wrong as I started crying during our long hug, and I told her. She listened and held me as I wept like a child in her arms.

I told her the darkest details as I was sitting on the bed, crying my eyes out. I told her that Ron took his life and how I was left here to figure everything out on my own. I can't recall if I shared how he broke my heart and beat me down. She reassured me that God has a plan, and she provided a sense of comfort that was indescribable.

Between the brain fog of grief and trauma of hearing, smelling, and feeling the vibration of someone's life slip away, running into my friend was everything I needed at that moment. I needed her to tell me everything was going to be okay, her prayers, her hug, her strength, and her hope. God knew I needed her presence, so he placed her in my path. I knew everything would be okay.

I reunited with my friends, and they were amazed that someone who lives three hours away was randomly in Ventura at the same time as us. Our little day trip was planned at the last minute, and in the blink of an eye, I might have missed my friend and his son walking along the beach. This was one of the many signs from God that things would be okay, and that I would make it through.

PICKING UP HIS ASHES

A few days later, I got a call from the mortuary, and it was time for my husband to be picked up. I wanted the last physical place for Ron's body to visit to be somewhere he enjoyed, so I found a mortuary in Kernville. My sister and I hopped in the car, and our journey began. I was in such a survival state, I can't recall much. But I do remember when we pulled into the parking lot to pick up my late husband's ashes, "Come Sail Away" by Styx came on the radio. I began crying immediately. He had sailed away, and now it was time for my ship to set sail—for a new chapter to begin.

My sister wanted to make things a little brighter, so we stopped at Costco on our way home. This big box store always brought a smile to my face. We decided it was the perfect opportunity to add her to the membership. Member services told me that since the main membership was in my deceased husband's name, I needed to bring his death certificate. Feeling more defeated than ever, we walked back out to the car, and I showed the paper copy that confirmed my husband was no longer living. I cannot recall if I bought anything that trip, but I know I left without a grin.

13 THE ANNOUNCEMENT

Two weeks ago, I lost my adventure buddy, my best friend, and the love of my life—my husband. I kept hoping I'd wake up from this horrible nightmare and that you would be back by my side.

No words can take away this pain, comfort me, or bring you back. We were so close to jumping into the next chapter of our lives. Thank you for always helping me seek joy, adventure, and God in our lives. I hope to be reunited with you in heaven. Meanwhile, enjoy the view from up there. I hope you have the most beautiful A-frame and please keep sending Godwinks, so I know you're still with me.

Make sure to tell the people around you that you love them and give them extra hugs. Be kind to people. We truly never know the battles in another person's head.

Seal in the Desert

Please send over your favorite Bible verse, prayers, and encouraging songs, to theprayerbus@gmail.com... I'm still trying to scramble the shattered pieces together.

I've been using this time to grow closer to God, and am truly relying on His strength.

If you or anyone you know is struggling with depression, here is the suicide prevention line: 800-273-8255 #theprayerbus

These are the words I used to tell the world my husband no longer existed on this earth. The days I had to myself made a huge difference in my healing journey. I was able to process and focus on myself.

I will never forget coordinating with his mom how we would share this news. We realized she was blocked from my Facebook profile—that anything I would share, she would not see. That was another barrier most people don't need to deal with. I figured out how to unblock her and the rest of the family, and then it was time to tell the world.

Why was his family blocked from all of social media? Ron had blocked his family after he got in a fight when he visited them and disagreed over political beliefs. In the middle of the night, when he got home from visiting them, he took my phone and did some magic with it. There was no arguing with Ron, especially when he mentioned details from his childhood that may have justified his ability to cut off his family. So, like the "good wife" I was, I let it sit and did not reach out to his family or fight back and tell him he needed to make up with them.

I did not realize at the moment this was an excuse for him to self-isolate. It would make the move away from family much easier as he could just forget the people who raised him. I believe the fight happened in October or November of 2020. So, we did not spend the holidays with his family. If I recall correctly, he tried talking on the phone with his family a few times before our big planned move out of state.

I made sure to tell all of his friends and closest family before I publicly announced Ron's death. While I was processing losing my husband and the trauma it entailed, I was also trying to tread lightly on breaking other people's hearts. I'll never forget his best friend thought I was him…trying to reach out. I just wanted to tell his friend he was no longer here. In retrospect, it probably would have been easier to just text and say, his friend is dead. But he deserved more.

I never wanted his best friend to think or regret that the argument that they got in might have played a role in Ron taking his life. I have battled and worked so hard to convince myself that Ron taking his life was his choice. At the end of the day I did everything in my strength and willpower to stop him. Texting someone that their friend —whether in an argument or not—killed themself is not quite the best way to deliver that news.

I decided to deliver it differently. I waited for him to be able to talk over the phone. At that moment, he thought Ron was the one writing the text to him—asking for forgiveness. Never realizing he had already left this planet. His body was already being transported to the crematory, being burned to ashes, transported in his blue bag. The bag I touched as I tried to feel for his hand as I said goodbye for the last time.

As Ron was ragefully texting his friend, we were on our way to Kernville. I recall looking at him, and saying I really wanted him to be present and to spend time with me. He told his friend that he was on a date with his wife, and they might talk it through later. They never made up.

I waited two weeks before I told the world. A piece of figuring it out included how to unblock his family on Facebook and how to tag them in a status. What I posted was so honoring to Ron and included all of the beautiful details of him being my best friend. I had not yet reflected on how much he broke me until much later in my healing journey.

Sometimes, when we're able to take a step back and realize how broken we have become, we are able to see what has truly happened and how we have changed as people. I was always a strong woman, but I wish I would have realized how much I changed over time. How I grew apart from myself and how I grew into a different person. I relied entirely on my husband. I was codependent, and I thought I couldn't do this life without him. I suppose I was the seal in the desert. I was the one refusing to seek help, thinking the swimming pool I lived in was the life I deserved.

14 THE HEALING JOURNEY

June 29, 2021

When I first took this picture, I thought about how empty this truck looked. It felt like a metaphor for my life. I'm choosing to have God fill the void & truly guide me in each decision I make.

I knew God before but nothing like the relationship I have now. I wasn't the Christian God wanted me to be. Losing my husband has forced me to fully surrender to His love. And some beautiful things have been happening.

"My ears had heard of you, but now my eyes have seen you."

Job 42:5

Stay faithful, be kind, & tell your friends and family how much you love them.

When I first lost Ron, I felt completely empty. Although he broke me into pieces, he was my best friend. Ron was an incredible Christian—at least on the surface and in front of others. He was not always the best Christian to his wife. His actions to strangers drew me closer to God and closer to him. Sometimes, I wished that Ron would care about me as much as he cared about others and about his image as a Christian.

In retrospect, if he did not help me become the Christian that I am, I would be in a whole different place and mindset. I had to become completely dependent on God. Throughout this process, I learned that giving up your life and leaving all things in God's hands is so fulfilling. I have had the opportunity to step back and truly see God move in my life. I recognize the little blessings that I would take for granted previously.

While Ron was an incredible Christian, we never made our way to church for Wednesday night services. He was always so tired because of work. After losing Ron, and not having any time constraints, I chose to start going on Wednesdays. I felt God move in me like never before. I was constantly convicted and grew closer to God on those nights. The church I attended was a quiet, conservative, tucked away place in the middle of the mountains. I did not mind the drive because it was the same distance from the off-grid property to church as it was from my parents' house. Instead of listening to my husband yell at me on the drive, I listened to music and sang as loudly as I wanted to. I got to enjoy mountain drives, and I would often notice hawks flying above me on my way to worship God.

There has been a plethora of breathtaking moments in which I truly have experienced God. Most of them have revolved around nature. When we open our eyes and become aware of the world around us, the more we will see the love and joy that is just waiting to be poured into our lives.

July 8, 2021

This was supposed to be a happy picture. It was when I took it. The next day life changed forever. One month ago, a piece of me stopped breathing. My husband succumbed to his bipolar and depression. I originally thought about getting rid of the bus and just running away. But God had different plans. I was sent a free generator, someone donated solar panels to me, & I found a blue hot wheels bus (We used to collect hot wheels). God was shouting, "KEEP GOING!".

My husband wanted to name it the Prayer Bus. I recorded a video of him sharing all of the Godwinks (reasons) we were going to call it The Prayer Bus. [Stay tuned as I'll post the video eventually].

There have been several people God put in my path who have shared how suicide changed their life or how they've contemplated it. Can we please normalize talking about our feelings, pressing into God, asking for help, and attending therapy?

One day—when I'm ready—I will build The Prayer Bus and spread some hope. Do I know anything about building a bus— absolutely not! But I know God will provide the skills or people to help. The bus is already painted & seats have been removed. If you have any #skoolie tips, registration in CA, a place to park & build near Santa Clarita, or insurance tips, please reach out.

Seal in the Desert

When I wrote this post, I was unsure whether
or not the bus would still work. After all, we bought a bus
that had over three-hundred thousand miles, which is a
pretty stupid idea even though they last forever. I avoided
going to the off-grid property because it was the last place
I saw Ron, and it brought back the memories of trauma I
constantly tried to suppress.

Just one month after losing Ron, I was already
feeling lighter. It probably was not apparent in this post.
But I was beginning to realize I spent the last several years
living in survival mode. While Ron was by my side, I was
not able to breathe, share my opinions, or express myself. I
was in a very sad place, and being released from a toxic
marriage brought some freedom, albeit not in the way I
could have ever imagined.

Losing Ron was undeniably the worst thing that
could have ever happened in my life. No one goes into a
marriage and hopes that one day they will become a
widow. No one has any expectations for someone after
they lose a loved one. In fact, several people told me to
"not make any big decisions for the first year". I am
choosing to shatter that expectation and focus on myself.

There have been beautiful circumstances I've come across while prioritizing myself.

Instead of running away and crawling into the deep hole, I decided to seek out ways I might see Ron. Walking down the hot wheels aisle with my sister was challenging. But when I saw the blue bus, I knew it was a sign. When I got the free generator and solar panels donated, I knew it was an opportunity for me to pursue this bus dream.

Some of the last footage I have of Ron was all of the Godwinks and reasons why we were going to name the bus the Prayer Bus. The video can be found on my YouTube under "Forever Changed and the Prayer Bus". There were several reasons to call it the Prayer Bus. At first, I was hesitant thinking that others might perceive us as traveling missionaries—which was not our intention. But considering everything that happened, I'm choosing to continue on with this name and the journey has become even more beautiful. I have had a village of friends and family step up and offer to help. One friend offered to take the bus to his property and work on building it into the tiny home of my dreams. He recalled that if the situation was reversed, Ron would do the same.

Seal in the Desert

Through sharing my story, several people have shared their experiences with suicide, how they lost a brother, a sister, a friend, a daughter, or a son. There is such a shame in talking about suicide, perhaps because it makes people uncomfortable. We never want to inconvenience others, and vulnerability is a trait that is often hard to find and even more challenging to live by. With all these things taken into account, why would anyone choose to talk about this?

I've made it my mission to share my feelings, my journey—the highs and the lows—and talk about how therapy healed me. Since this post, I can confirm that the Prayer Bus is a go, and it will be built and spread hope. I look forward to the journey and healing it will bring about in the lives of everyone I run into as well as my own.

PICKING UP THE SHATTERED PIECES

My friends always knew me as the hyper-productive person growing up. I was a workaholic. I think the biggest appeal to my relationship with Ron was he offered a different perspective on life. He made me feel it was okay to take vacation days. To slow down, breathe, and see the nature around me. Naturally with him gone, a huge piece of me was missing. My friends were rightfully worried. Even though they saw how miserable I was with Ron, they wanted my mind to be in the right place moving forward.

I had officially resigned from my job, less than a week before Ron took his life. I was not in the place to go begging for my dream job back. Also, one of my closest friends was going to fill the position. But most of all, I was not ready to be humbled by people always giving me the sad, empathetic stare. I did not want my traumatic, life-changing event to be what I was recognized for. I wanted a fresh start.

Let's rewind for a moment my job for the past two years was an instructional coach. Pieces of my job included modeling lessons with teachers, working in one-on-one coaching cycles, planning professional development for teachers, and analyzing school-wide data to support student learning. In the moment, stepping back into a traditional classroom was not an option for me. I was not sure if something simple might trigger me, and I was unsure how my mental health would progress throughout each new season of being a widow. I was not even sure how my brain would function when trying to manage a classroom.

I began looking into substitute teaching. I started gathering information to apply as a substitute in the school district closest to me. But as I have come to realize with so much of my life, God had other plans.

My friend told me about an interesting position that opened up at the district I was thinking of applying to work at as a substitute. It was called an "instructional coach" position for a teacher on special assignment. Ironically, this was the position I had in my last school district. So, I pivoted, and instead of gathering materials to apply for substitute teaching, I began crafting my resume and my application for the instructional coach position.

I recalled a consultant who I had the opportunity to work with at my previous school district also collaborated with the school district I was applying for. So, I reached out to her and told her my story. She put in a great recommendation for me at the new school district. Originally, I was unsure if I was even qualified for the position or if I would mentally be ready to take on a new job. Moving to a new school district, there are new programs, new names, new procedures, and new normals to navigate. But I decided to still give it a go.

Within less than two weeks after the conversation with my friend, I clicked submit on my application with my letters of recommendation. First and foremost I need to thank my therapist, for pushing me to apply for the job. She was alongside me the whole time and helped me gain the confidence I needed. In addition, my friend who worked for the school district helped me determine this was something that I was qualified for, and that I could bring about positive change in the district.

I got a call about my application, and an interview was scheduled. So, less than one month after Ron took his life—on July 7th—I interviewed for a new position. As I was driving to the interview, I heard God whisper to me. He said, "Heather, if you gain the confidence to speak in front of all these new faces you don't know, then you will be more prepared to be a motivational speaker in the future."

I jumped into the interview. It was the first time I got dressed up in a while, and I used my sister's makeup because I did not have any at the time. I styled my hair very interesting the night before to result in curls as I was sleeping. I let my long hair loose before the interview, and it felt good to look put together.

When I walked into the district office, I found a familiar face at the front desk, a parent who used to volunteer regularly at the local park I once worked at. I found out she was just filling in for the day, and I realized this was undoubtedly another Godwink. We did not talk about my life circumstances as I was trying to keep my game face and be ready for an interview.

Then, it was time for the interview. I walked up to the meeting room and was introduced to several principals and a few other pivotal people who would determine if I was capable of landing this position. After introductions, they mentioned they were all vaccinated, and we could take off our masks if I was comfortable. At this time, I still was not vaccinated—as Ron was very against it. I was honest and said, "I'm not vaccinated," and we all kept our masks on throughout the interview.

I was so grateful that I told the truth, as keeping my mask on really came in handy when I was asked the question: "Is there anything we might not know about you that you would like to tell us?"

I never felt my mouth make so many different facial expressions at once. Thankfully the mask hid these reactions. For about twenty seconds, I debated whether I should disclose that I was recently a widow, and looking for the opportunity to start over, pondering if I should share that I desire to build a new life—a second chance.

I said that although I had never taught in the town or went through the school system, I loved serving the community through my work with Parks and Recreation. I felt this was a safer answer, and they would not question my capacity to be a district leader. I was then asked if I had any questions, and I asked about coaching confidentiality as this is a key component of being an instructional coach. I thanked them for the interview and was walked downstairs.

In the short walk downstairs, I was asked whether I lived in locally, and I answered yes, and that I might relocate to a peaceful place in the hills between Castaic and Lancaster—Green Valley or Lake Elizabeth because housing there is much more affordable. I was told they would make a decision by the end of the week, and I would get a phone call.

I walked out of the building filled with self-loathing. How could I get a position as an instructional coach without showing my smile? Why did I not lie about the vaccinated situation? This school district seems very tight-knit, and I'm an outsider; there is no way I will get this. I rated myself a six out of ten on the interview and accepted my fate that this was not meant to be. But after a while, I was happy that I tried, I logged into teletherapy, and I told my therapist. She told me it was a huge step to even go in for an interview less than a month after losing my husband.

She was right. Then I noticed my phone ringing. I answered and was told that they were in the process of checking in with all of my references. I was asked if the best phone numbers to reach them were provided—because not everyone is always at school during the summer. I was told my references should be expecting a call. I got off the phone call, and I jumped up and down a few times. This was the win that I needed. My therapist told me she was proud of me, and I suppose that is one of the times that I realized my self-doubt was not the piece of me that would control my future.

My negative image, and the person who reinforced that was gone, and it was now time to start reinventing myself and allowing my brain to function again.

I was and am capable of great things. That's a big reason why I'm telling this story. I hope you never doubt your ability to grow, change, and you choose to challenge the beliefs you have about yourself.

Seal in the Desert

July 17, 2021

I've always tried to give off this very strong persona. I was always a happy kid. I never experienced anything that I couldn't handle. I can pretend like everyday I'm completely okay, but that's not the story. I've given this mountain to God, and I'm relying on His strength and grace. But there's a couple pieces I haven't shown through this journey of grieving.

•My brain isn't the same, and I HATE that. Multi-tasking makes my head spin. I can't retain things like I used to.

•I haven't cooked in over a month, and I have no desire to. I've been living off of snacks.

•I still don't feel like eating most of the time. My friends & family will force me to eat. I mostly enjoy the company, but the food is helpful too.

•Flashbacks and memories appear out of nowhere. Sometimes they bring a smile to my face. Other times, I get pissed, or I cry.

•Losing your best friend and husband suddenly leaves a void that words can't describe. There's no one to tell your day to. No one to share affection or cuddling with, and it's horrible.

You matter. Your life is so valuable, and even when you're feeling the deepest lows, remember your life matters. Please tell people how much they mean to you.

#sunrise #reflect #widow #grief #griefjourney

The strength that I felt I exemplified was in fact my greatest kryptonite. I chose to pretend everything was okay, and I'm here to share that it's okay to not be okay. Your greatest strength should not entail shielding yourself from the world and hiding your secrets from the people who love you and can help you.

It's okay if you're not happy everyday; people will still recognize your value. It's okay to ask for help and to admit you're still a work in progress. I chose to give this journey to God, and that has been the best decision I've made in this lifetime.

There is a song that comes to mind as I'm reflecting on this post. It's called "I Can't Carry This Anymore" by Anson Seabra. We are not built to carry things all to ourselves—that's the beauty in sharing our journey.

I'm writing these words six months after I posted this on Instagram, and there are some pieces that ring true. My short-term memory will never be the same. I am slightly better at multi-tasking; however, I write everything down to ensure that I don't forget an important detail or miss something. Inevitably, I still forget things, and my brain is forever altered from the trauma.

Seal in the Desert

Nevertheless, I have accepted this and given myself grace.
I will keep trying to grow my brain, and because of
neuroplasticity, I am capable of it. I have noticed the
progress in the past six months, and I'm proud of it.

Six months ago, I could barely cook, and I still
did not have much of an appetite. I have survived from
Fairlife chocolate milk, and Premier Protein shakes and
bars. I also enjoyed pistachios, crunchy rice rollers, and
rotisserie chicken from Costco. This is what my meals
mostly entailed.

I began going to the gym in late June and was
forced to start eating more consistently. I did not want to
be the fat chick in the gym who passed out because she
wasn't eating enough food. I recall there were some
instances when I would be hitting the punching bag, and I
had to cool down for a little. I knew that almost fainting
was not my objective at the gym. My goal was to improve
my mental health. As I learned about working out, I
learned that fueling my body was the only way I could
make physical progress.

Through therapy and my life experiences I
have learned to tune out some of the flashbacks a little
better. I understand that the memories I have are a piece

of me that will forever be a part of my past. But I know
these experiences are not the defining piece of my future.

I know at the end of the day, I did everything in
my power to stop him, but it doesn't take away the fact
that I was there. What I have learned throughout this
journey is that a best friend is not someone who destroys
you and breaks you down. Someone who loves you would
never treat you this way.

For a while, I felt very lonely. I would crave the
affection and attention, but I knew I could not just replace
Ron. That was not fair for myself. I needed to process
everything. Through this time of reflection, I have learned
a lot. When we are brave enough to acknowledge our
trauma, and the things that have broken us—head on—we
can gain mental clarity and begin to grow. Sometimes it
might feel like we're stumbling forward— as it did six
months ago. Keep doing the work, slowly, and you will
inch forward and begin to feel like yourself again. Or
perhaps you will begin to discover a new version of
yourself. A healed version that craves peace and
authenticity.

15 THE CELEBRATION OF LIFE

As with death, comes a funeral. A time to lay your loved one to rest. Funerals are different from most life events. At a birthday party or a wedding, you can anticipate how many people will arrive because you have a specific guest list. However, with funerals, how can you tell someone they are not allowed to be there? Someone who may have had a meaningful purpose in the dead person's life. I could not limit this, and planning a funeral with a very vague idea of who might attend is challenging.

I had several of my colleagues who wanted to attend. These beautiful people wanted to be there to support me. I didn't want people to see me so broken. The girl who smiled through everything who hid all the pain. It simply wasn't fair for people to experience that side of Heather. But truthfully, I was not ready for people to see how hurt I was.

A few days before the funeral, I had Costco flowers delivered to his mom's house. We had a time when all of the family came together, and we created floral arrangements for the funeral. The irony in this is less than three years earlier—this is what my bridesmaids and I did together for the ceremony that was supposed to intertwine our lives together forever.

The pastor who said Ron's funeral baptized us together, at the end of summer in 2020. Meeting with the pastor and telling him more about Ron was challenging. We were these people who quietly attended the church but chose not to connect with others. After all, we thought we were moving across the country, and why would we bother building friendships? Another big reason for not getting connected was the groups met on weeknights, and far drive.

I did not want anyone to see my brokenness. I chose not to connect because I realized the people who knew me might notice the tear stains I wore after being berated by Ron on the forty-five minute drive. I did not want anyone to see my brokenness. In hindsight, I wish I would have let the people at church see my pain. Maybe we would have sought counseling together. Perhaps the urn would not have been the end journey that Ron ended up on.

Back to the funeral—his mother, grandma and I coordinated pictures and collages as well as bookmarks. I had a really challenging time making any decisions. Planning a funeral for your husband in your twenties is never something that anyone has on their bucket list. It was through God's strength and all of my friends' prayers that I was able to make it through this time.

The pastor delivered a beautiful message. Ron's dad said a wonderful eulogy, and I believe my dad spoke too. Then it was time for the microphone to be opened for anyone to share. There were about twenty people from his work who attended the funeral. Several of the men he worked with spoke about him. They mentioned that he was always encouraging and that he was such a positive person. One of his colleagues said he nicknamed Ron "Rejoice" because that was the spirit he always had. He did not know that Ron was a Christian at the time, but he said it was obvious by the way he acted.

None of Ron's coworkers knew how much he complained about work to me. But I was grateful to have their presence and words shared about how he motivated them.

Several of my friends in the room—who heard the true story, and saw me crumble—realized that the light Ron radiated onto others was the light he stole from me. The situation reminds me of the song "Robin Hood" by Anson Seabra. I heard this when he was alive, and I will never forget how much I cried. I knew he was depleting my light, but there was no safe emergency exit I could turn to.

One friend spoke and reminded us how Ron would always give the tightest squeezing hugs—the ones where he would try to pick you up. Ron loved hugs, and one of the things I truly appreciated about him was the way he would hold me tightly in his loving embrace when I was having a hard day. The friend also mentioned how at the end of every phone call, he would say, "love you." He understood that Ron's love for others was deep.

When planning for the wedding, I waited until the last moment to plan my vows. Similarly, I waited until the last minute to plan the words I would say for the funeral. I was not sure if I would have the courage to speak my heart. No one anticipated the newly widowed wife to say her goodbyes and thank yous from the pulpit. However, I chose to. As the line of people wanting to share their memories of Ron lulled, I choked up the courage to walk up and share a little bit about him.

On our way to the funeral, my family and I saw a deer. This was my Godwink or my way of knowing that I had to get up there and share. After finding the courage to walk up, I introduced myself and told others this deer reminded me of the freedom that Ron now has. That he is free from his depression and the sad pieces that held him down. I reminded everyone that Ron would want us to live with God in the forefront of everything we do and to treat others with kindness.

We ended the ceremony and had the reception. It was overwhelming how many hugs I got. I am thankful for everyone's lackluster attitude towards COVID on the day of the memorial. We did not need to wear our masks, and we were not worried about social distancing. I have heard horror stories of many families and friends who waited for months to bury the people they loved as a result of the pandemic. I am grateful this was one piece of the equation I did not need to deal with.

I was approached by a family member at the end of the ceremony who told me that Ron was tortured as a child and that he was always worried about me.

What broke me was the fact that I found out about his manic after he passed. I wish I would have known when Ron was in a manic phase. I did not realize it was a part of his bipolar diagnosis. If I would have known the signs of it, and that it was something Ron did not have control over, perhaps I could have tried to react differently. I can't go back and change the past, so I will keep the things I have learned close to my heart as I navigate forward in this life.

16 STUMBLING FORWARD

July 26, 2021

For a moment the other day, I felt like I wasted summer. Then I remembered all of the beautiful people who've lifted my spirits, grabbed a drink with me, joined me at church, brought me to the beach, met me for food, and forced me to get OUT. I've been intentionally choosing NOT to just lay in bed because I don't see the Godwinks inside the walls.

•••

This summer has been challenging, but all of your prayers, texts, calls, messages, love, and support have been getting me through. Thank you for helping me rediscover myself and find happiness in the little things.

I'm choosing to honor the gift of life by living. 🖤
#living #suicideprevention #suicideawarness #life

When you have a moment in life, where the ocean overtakes you, and then you're pulled down by the current and you are grasping for a breath of fresh air, fighting to get up—that is when you must call on your lifesavers.

I had an army of lifesavers willing to spend time with me and assist in me rediscovering myself. These people helped me push past the trauma I experienced and helped me to truly understand that in the little everyday blessings, we can find happiness. All of my friends were by my side during the dark times—when I would hear an ambulance or fire truck and shake, when the bursts of fireworks triggered me, and when I was sucked into the abyss of sadness.

The summer of 2021 was everything but wasted. It was the time that I needed to find out who I am. There are no words that can describe the gift of time my friends gave me over these months. I am eternally grateful for their companionship, listening ears, and willingness to stay by my side. Thank you for hearing my tough stories. Thank you for wanting to come to the funeral—even if you did not know Ron. Thank you for wanting to start a

Seal in the Desert

Go Fund Me. Thank you for collecting money without even asking. Thank you for sending the meals and for your companionship. But most of all, thank you for your prayers and checking in.

There are so many people that helped on this journey, but I would not be here, writing these words without three people. My sister and my two best friends.

My sister encouraged me to start going to the gym which was my way of letting out my anger and frustration. I found peace with the punching bag. She pushed me to become a better person, physically and emotionally. Without my sister, I have no clue where I would be. Maybe I would still be in the dark room, refusing to eat. Maybe I would be off traveling by myself. All I know is I am happy she stepped up and helped me in this healing process. I could not have done it without her.

My best friend spent hours with me, and although she refused to be my therapist, she is my voice of reason and often helps me think about things in a different way. She gave me the ability to reframe things and really advocated for me to go to therapy. Within less than a month, we went to San Diego for a birthday trip, and she made me laugh countless times. She challenged my painful thoughts and reminded me that I have the ability to rewrite some of the tougher memories I have.

One time, I told her I did not think I would be capable of having kids in the future and how I did not want to pass on my trauma to them. I will never forget how she yelled at me while sharing that the experiences and the healing I have chosen will be an incredible way for me to pass strength and resilience onto my future offspring. When you find a friend that helps you grow emotionally and mentally, never ever let go.

Another one of my best friends truly resurfaced. When I was married to Ron, he did not like her. We went to several concerts together, and she always brought out the fun, carefree side of me. Thank you for meeting me in the Walgreens parking lot, less than a week after losing Ron. Thank you for giving me the biggest hug and letting me know things will be okay. Thank you for having me over. Thank you for blasting Coldplay and encouraging me to sing along—several glasses of wine deep. Thank you for making me feel a sense of true happiness again.

Thank you for doing this all when you were dealing with your own challenges. Growing up as neighbors, with our secret handshakes was always fun. However, growing together, with life's biggest changes and challenges is one of the biggest blessings we could do as best friends. I am so happy God chose our parents to be neighbors, and that despite Ron hating you, you came back to me. Thank you for being a true best friend.

July 29, 2021

With marriage, two people become one, and you never anticipate that bond will be broken. The past few years I grew into a wife, but I never realized how much I changed. This summer has given me the chance to figure out who I am and what I enjoy. I wish I could say I know who I am as a person again, but that's going to take lots of time. So, what's been keeping me going? God, therapy, friends, the gym, the lake, local breweries, my dogs, and living in the moment.

Don't take any moments for granted and keep growing to discover the purpose God has for you.

PS. Reach out to at least 3 friends or family and share how much they mean to you and how much you love them.

Marriage is undoubtedly beautiful and the goal of it is to unite two people. Nothing is healthy about completely transforming into the other person. I lost myself while married to Ron, so when he left this earth, I had no clue who I was. I am still discovering the things that bring a smile to my face. One of the most important things I have learned about myself along the way is not to hide behind a mask. The courage to be vulnerable has been one of my biggest strengths. When I am willing to share about my hardships, I open myself to growing beautiful friendships and connections with others.

One time I was on the phone with my best friend and Ron began yelling at me for leaving five-gallon water jugs on the front lawn to dry. He was concerned that someone was going to steal them. In the middle of his tantrum, I sadly told my friend I had to go. My mom reminded me of a time when Ron and I were getting ready to leave for a trip, and how he asked me to check the tire pressure. I told him I did not know how. He began to berate me and question how I did not know how to do such a thing. He was also upset that I put the bikes in the trailer and made me move them from the trailer to the back of the truck. Everything had to be his way.

Marriage is not slavery. Nor should it ever feel like that. It should be a blend of two people. In my opinion, the two people should grow together and feel comfortable talking about anything in their hearts. I imagine marriage as a beautiful blending of souls that still have their individual identity but that choose to come together and be a home for one another.

In retrospect, the summer of 2021 was exactly what I needed. Even on the hard days I chose to chase the sunlight, get out of bed, and move my body. These slow movements helped me inch forward and grow into the person that I have become today. I hope we can all find the courage to grow into exactly who we are meant to be. Exploring the pain we have endured is so worthwhile.

Seal in the Desert

August 12, 2021

It's been two months.

The longest, most dragged out two months of my life. I've learned more about myself in these past two months. I've been going to the gym, so I can eat more consistently, and it's somewhat working. I've felt happiness, but I've also felt extreme loneliness and sadness. Overall, I've had more consistency than I've had in a long time. I'm not concerned about walking on eggshells everyday or being yelled at for something minuscule. I'm continuing to learn who I am as a person and setting huge boundaries.

Grief isn't a straight line, and the stupidest things will break you on days. Sometimes I catch myself staring off into the abyss of sadness. I've noticed the things that I thought were little things make a huge difference: staying grounded in God, talking to friends & therapy. Andy Grammar sings a song, "Wish You Pain" While I never ever wish anyone the heartbreak and wreckage that has become my story…I do hope that through the challenges we can all learn to grow and continue breathing. This pain has become a crucible that is forcing me to grow in ways I never imagined possible.

#widow #wishyoupain #growth #keepgoing #mentalhealth #mentalhealthawareness

I shared how I was still struggling with eating in this post. A huge challenge I experienced as a result of losing Ron was shedding some pounds and this could have easily spiraled into an eating disorder because I hated my body image. My first steps into the gym began to break the idea that eating was bad, and I began to realize that food is not only good for your body but also for your soul. On Tuesdays and Fridays, my dad and I would enjoy tacos or quesadillas from the taco stand up the street. Although it was not the healthiest, I knew it was a consistent and delicious meal I would always savor. In addition to my journey with food, I began to lift and strength train. Although I had no clue what I was doing, I had a routine, which was very helpful.

As I posted this picture, I admitted for the first time—on social media—that I felt consistency. I had several people reach out to me and share that they could relate to walking on eggshells. My heart breaks for the people of this world who navigate this life with such precision, trying not to poke the bear. Love is not about tiptoeing your way around another, so you can make them happy. You should feel free enough to speak your mind and to be yourself—two things I never experienced in my marriage.

The boundaries that I set were mostly in reference to any potential future relationships. I knew I had to take care of myself—mentally, emotionally, and spiritually. In order to do this, I decided it was important to truly get to know others first. I set very firm boundaries for dating, and it helped me discover and build my self-worth. Boundaries are not something meant for others to break down, but rather can help you to build yourself up and keep yourself safe. Boundaries are not walls and there is a vast difference between both. Walls we put up to block others out and to feel sheltered. Boundaries are the line that we don't allow others to cross. I never had boundaries previously, and exercising my self-worth through my boundaries has been a huge step in my healing process.

Choosing to continue to breathe can be challenging on some days. Some days feel like I am merely surviving, and that's why I have tried to find my purpose not only in myself. Knowing that I had a story to tell, and that I might be able to help someone else, makes all of my darkest days worth it.

Pain is interesting. We can choose to hold onto it, and it will undoubtedly suffocate us, and morph us into the ugliest version of ourselves. I have chosen to grow from my pain. I know these circumstances are not what will define me for eternity, but rather the strength I gain from them is what will be my driving force.

Seal in the Desert

August 19, 2021

I'm celebrating finding myself again.

Having someone help me rephrase my negative and sad thoughts into positives is simply beautiful. Surprisingly, I almost thought I didn't need to go to therapy after my world turned upside down. But my best friend helped me sign up, and I am so grateful. I've learned so much about myself. If you've been through challenging times, therapy is definitely an incredible way to grow through the pain and can help you crawl out of the dark hole.

Reach out to a few family and friends today and tell them how much they mean to you.

#findingyourself #widow #suicideprevention #mentalhealth #therapy #mentalhealthmatters #growthmindset

I am still mind-blown by the fact I thought I might not need therapy. I failed at preventing my husband from killing himself, and then I tried to perform CPR on his dead body. If that does not qualify you for therapy, I do not know what will. Taking the first step and admitting you need help and need time for yourself is essential.

My therapist helped me to acknowledge my negative self-talk and realize that when I start to spiral, I need to name my emotion, sit with it, and then move past it. Moving past the negative emotions is not easy. I am so grateful I took the leap of faith to sign up and to explore the darkness. I am a firm believer that everyone should attend some type of therapy to process the challenges life throws at them.

Sitting with a therapist, I had the opportunity to be heard. Most sessions we would talk about how I was feeling. She would ask me clarifying questions about my emotions and the way I saw situations. She helped me to understand that many of the experiences I had were unacceptable and demoralizing. A therapist offers a new set of eyes. They are here to listen to your truth and to help you find the most authentic version of yourself.

THE LONELY ANNIVERSARY

August 25, 2021

I never anticipated this picture of the dogs & I would be the story I tell. Here are some of my favorite memories from 3 years ago and from the biggest party of my life. Ron was constantly growing: closer to God, quitting drinking and smoking, and in his ambitions. I loved that about him. He had a drive to be better. He finally convinced me to sell the house & live off-grid in 160 square feet. He taught me how to live SIMPLE.

We made a lot of beautiful memories, and I will forever hold those close to my heart. I made quite a few sacrifices. That's what I thought marriage was. Giving up yourself to complete someone else.

I watched as my friendships were slowly picked away at until the only friend I was allowed to rely on was him. I was pushed to the darkest depths where I thought I would never be able to crawl out of. The words you told me in your times of anger are burned into my essence as a being. I'm not sure how I withstood so much, but I'm glad I'm still here.

I ignored all of the warning signs. I'm sorry I let you down. I'm sorry I didn't force you to go to therapy. I'm sorry for losing myself and not being able to continue giving you endless hope. I'm sorry I wasn't strong enough to stop you.

I'm glad you are at peace and out of pain. Now it's time for me to continue working on healing & seeking peace.

I'll continue speaking out about mental health in your and my honor. I'll ask how people are really doing and try to be a place for people to share how they're feeling.

You'll always be in the pieces of my heart that you shattered. #widow #anniversary #suicideawarness #mentalhealth #mentalhealthmatters

Wow, going back and reading this post moves me to tears. I shared a few pictures from the wedding and shared these words on what would have been our three-year anniversary. We truly had some great memories together, and Ron tried to grow into the best person he could be. I admired his drive to better himself, but it seemed with each step he took to improve himself, he found different ways to belittle me. He chipped away at my identity until I no longer recognized the woman in the mirror—which is ironic because for a while we did not have a mirror in our tiny home.

The sacrifices that I made were countless. Not going out with friends, so I could cook him dinner. Quitting my job to pursue a simpler life that would help his mental health. Not talking to my friends or family during our coveted time together.

Marriage is not giving up on yourself to water someone else. You need to take time to water your roots, so you can bring the truest version of you to the world and your relationship. No matter what, I promise I will never give up on myself again. I will keep my eyes on the image in the mirror and make sure I stay strong and true to myself. You deserve self-love too, and if you don't make time or effort to love yourself, you cannot truly give love.

Like most bad memories, I have been able to repress the horrible putdowns Ron told me that ruined my self-worth. I have chosen to rewrite the narrative that he told me in his fits of anger. I have gotten better at loving myself. Since Ron has left this world, I have learned my value. When I'm told I'm beautiful or a good kisser, I reflect on how my husband told me the exact opposite of both of those things. I was not enough. I was never enough for him. He broke me down into so many pieces hoping that I would be filled with so much self-loathing and never try to be in a future relationship.

I am glad I persisted, and if you are a victim of verbal, mental, or emotional abuse, I know you can persist too. You deserve so much more. Learn from my mistakes and do not ignore the warning signs that are absolutely apparent. Keep your independence and do not allow yourself to fall into the darkness of someone who shadows your glow.

I have discovered some of Brene Brown's incredible literature, and in *Braving the Wilderness*, she talks about being rejected by family and how we might deal with the pain. We can deny the pain, pass it along to others, or grow through our pain. I highly encourage reading her book and checking out her podcasts as they have helped me tremendously. I wish I had discovered her sooner. I might not have allowed myself to get so lost. Ron passed his pain along to me, and I am choosing to take that pain and explore it. Pain changes us, but we have the choice to grow through it and let it change us for the better. On the other hand, we can ignore our pain and then continue to hurt those around us.

I ended this post with the idea that Ron will always be in the pieces of my heart that he shattered. These words ring true months after losing him. I still see him all around me. I see him whenever I see an owl or a hawk, and I know he is at peace. I know he would want me to rebuild and to find myself again.

I do not think Ron's intention was ever to break me. However, in the breaking, it is easy to rebuild someone to be exactly what you want. I know for certain he wanted to shape me into his idea of a life partner. The biggest problem and blessing is he did not rebuild me. *I am rebuilding myself.*

Although I was a seal in the desert, that will not seal my destiny. He gave me the most beautiful gift I could have asked for: indescribable pain that I can grow through. He gave me the toughest years of my life. Moving forward, I will only seek peace and things that bring my heart joy. I am choosing to be selfish and know my worth. Without the rain, we can't experience the wildflowers. He was my rain, and while I was in a drought for a long time spring has come. Now, I am overflowing with flowers and new life.

I am in control of this narrative now, and I get to put back together the shattered pieces and grow into the most authentic, beautiful, and vulnerable version of myself.

August 27, 2021

Life is not a checklist

Life is NOT a checklist.

LIFE IS NOT A CHECKLIST.

This is one of the most important things I wish I believed 5 years ago.

- *You don't need to get married right away.*
- *You don't need to buy a house when you land your first career job.*
- *You probably won't have your dream job in your 20s.*
- *If you can't have kids because you're too old, there are so many other options.*

- *Don't rush things because you're trying to complete your checklist.*
- *This life ain't a scavenger hunt. So, quit running around trying to check the boxes, and just let God work things out.*

This is one of my favorite pieces of writing. My goal was to inspire others and help them to learn from my mistakes. But they also serve as a reminder to myself. I'm constantly reflecting on my daily actions, my past, and what my future might hold. Throughout this process of reflection, sometimes things get a bit muddled and I forget pieces that I have said. I also think my scatterbrained nature and forgetfulness is a result of my trauma, and the memories I try to suppress. Having a journal or a place to share my thoughts has been very helpful in processing everything I have experienced in my humble twenty-nine years of life.

So, back to the idea of living life as a checklist…I used to be very motivated by goals. I wanted to have a clear pathway of everything my future held and then make those things happen. Of course, being a cookie-cutter person is much easier when you're following a checklist, so naturally marriage, my dream job, a house, and kids were a piece of the checklist.

The first box I checked off was a very expensive one and came with a monthly payment that was a good chunk of my paycheck. However, I loved my house. I thought it would bring me joy, and I had Ron move in. It seemed like the perfect blend of things. What I never anticipated was how much I would miss my family and friends. I felt I left them behind when I moved an hour and a half away.

I thought the walls that surrounded me would bring together my family and friends; however, those exact walls were a facade. I was able to hide behind them. My friends and family did not want to come over because of the long drive and because Ron made them uncomfortable. They did not like the way he talked to me. Everything I hoped for in purchasing the house was gone. I might have checked the box, but it left me feeling empty.

The next piece on my checklist was the marriage box. I set a mental deadline and hoped Ron would propose within a year. Being a product of the Catholic private school system for thirteen years, I knew it was not socially acceptable to be living with a boyfriend. I thought being engaged would help that slightly, so we checked another box.

I got my dream job as an instructional coach, and this is one of the boxes I am most proud of. I got my Master's degree in education and I wanted to be able to make a difference across several classrooms. I loved building rapport with my students, but I wanted to inspire teachers and share strategies that would benefit more than my thirty students a year. So, I chose to leave the classroom and become a coach.

Ironically, the name of this book came about when I was coaching at a school. I was the youngest "teacher" on campus, and I felt like my impact was not to the extent it could have been. I felt like a seal, frying in the sun whenever I delivered training. I was told this was something we did fifteen years ago, but with a different name. Rightfully so, education recycles a lot of ideas.

I did not understand at the time that my job was the bow holding me together. I silently projected my pessimism from my marriage onto the job and the school I served. I was always the smiling teacher, and no one would ever anticipate I was hurting. I had some great memories with Ron, and in that moment, there was no way my lack of happiness could come from him. But upon reflection, I've discovered that my job was what kept me alive. Although I resigned from my job in June 2021, it was the first and only item from my checklist that I ran back to.

The next item on my checklist was having children. My friends remember me as the nanny who loved taking care of kids. I was the day camp counselor-turned-teacher to influence students to be hopeful and to see the world through a different perspective. From a very young age, I knew I wanted to have kids.

Then, I started to tell my friends I did not want children anymore; it was a heartbreaking decision. But I knew raising kids with him would have stemmed more pain and brokenness. Unfortunately, the bipolar, depression, and manic genes were passed down to Ron from his father's side for several generations. It was inevitable that if we had children, they would have these characteristics as well.

I hope from all of the words you have gathered throughout this book, you can sense I am a strong woman. However, I knew I was not strong enough to be a referee between arguments with my husband and any possible children we might have. I knew our offspring would possess the same genes, and I was not emotionally or mentally strong enough to deal with both him and any future children. So, I took natural steps to make sure we would never have children.

I would not be in the same place I currently am if Ron and I had a family. I am eternally grateful we chose not to. In fact, while we were living off-grid, for a quick moment, we debated whether we should start trying. Thank God I reminded him that we needed to have our roots planted first and a solid source of income before we began even considering children. Three dogs, a newborn, and an emotionally unstable husband would be too much within the walls of an eight and a half by twenty-foot tiny home.

Seal in the Desert

You might be wondering what path I am currently taking. In complete transparency, I have no clue. But I know when I trust God to work things out, I am so much stronger. I am not relying on items on a checklist as I move through life. In fact, I read Atomic Habits by James Clear, and I realized how detrimental goals can be. If we only focus on goals as the end means, we lose momentum. In this novel, James Clear shares how important it is for our identity to shape our life decisions and how the systems we create will help us achieve our goals.

The only checklist I am concerned about right now is how my mental health is doing. Am I growing? What does my heart truly need in this moment? I believe that everything the universe has planned for me will be revealed in its own timing. So yes, I am letting God work things out, and I have foregone the checklist.

September 1, 2021

I hope you never endure the suffering I've stumbled through.

I hope you find the one who truly loves you.

I hope you're able to endure the darkest nights.

I hope you're able to make it through the most challenging fights.

My hope is for you to keep growing

And never let that shine stop glowing.

Let your heart and your mind

Become beautifully intertwined.

Seek out the depths of your soul

Don't focus on the hole.

Please try to keep going.

Don't give up the fight,

And please shine your light.

It's okay for the sadness to be showing.

The tears wallowed up in your eyes.

They're not adding to your demise.

They're a healthy release if you let them flow.

Please just don't let yourself go.

#widow #grief #reflect #latenightthoughts #sleepless #keepgoing #growthroughwhatyougothrough

Seal in the Desert

I would be lying if I said I still do not have hard days. I can't always tell you where the hard days stem from. Typically, it is the compounding of several little events. Sometimes it will be a memory that pops up on Facebook, or someone saying the metaphor that they could shoot themselves. I don't have control over other people's words or actions, so for me, it is essential to be at peace with myself and take the time to breathe when I feel like the walls around me are caving in. During the most challenging times, I've always noticed that God will send several angels to check on me. It will be the random texts and calls that come through from my friends that always bring a smile to my face. But it is equally important for me to have the courage to reach out when I am feeling low.

My hope is that on the hard days you are reminded that you are loved and that you are worthy. Despite the darkness, I hope you still choose to shine. When I have dug deep into my soul, and explored the depths of it, I always notice a glow. A shine that is so bright it's blinding. Other people have pointed it out too, I think Brene Brown would refer to this as being wholehearted. I'm not afraid to hide behind my circumstances or the shame I have endured.

On some days, I still feel sad for no reason, and I realize when I wallow in my despair, I just feel emptier. However, when I have the courage to name my hurt and shame, I often feel much better and lighter. Sadness is not weakness. Tears are not childish or immature. Holding onto the dark memories we cling so tightly to within us will undoubtedly suffocate us. But when we have the strength and courage to unpack our trauma, memories, and things that seemingly add to our demise, we can gain wisdom and feel more whole than ever imagined.

A friend told me everything I have gone through will only make me a better, more relatable person and I began to think of life in that sense. Although I was dealt really crappy cards, and these are the events that have happened in my life, they do not define me.

We all go through hardships that shape us into the people we become. It is up to you to determine how your future will look, and how you can make it the best possible—despite the circumstances you've lived through.

THE FIRST HEAVENLY BIRTHDAY

January 29, 2022

Dear Heather,

I am sorry for stealing your sunlight. I am sorry for stealing the hope you had in this world. I am sorry for wanting to keep you from the world. I am sorry for all of the pain I put you through. I am sorry for the words I said that made you feel worthless. I am sorry for the never-ending heartache that I made you endure. I am sorry for the times when I hit our dogs. I am sorry for the times when I made you feel like you didn't want to be here anymore. I am sorry for breaking you and for every moment of pain I caused. I'm sorry that I'm no longer here to say these words to you. You deserved so much more.

I hope you find happiness in the little things that will replace the pieces of life that I stole from you. I know you will be able to smile. I know you will keep existing, and you will spread the light that this world deserves. The world needs you to keep going.

From your angel looking down upon you

Please don't allow yourself to be a seal in the desert.

ABOUT THE AUTHOR

Heather falls into a lot of categories. She is an educator,
dog mom, nature freak, obsessed with fitness, a nomad,
God-loving, and widow. Despite everything life has thrown
at her, she chooses to keep going and hopes you find the
courage to as well.

She has a podcast called Growing Resilient and can be
found on social media using #ThePrayerBus. She has also
published a poetry book called *Hurt, Healing, and Hope*. She
hopes to make this world a brighter place by bringing
awareness to mental health, self-care, and growing into the
most authentic version of herself.

She hopes the words in this book serve you and you always
find the courage to love yourself, speak up for yourself,
and never settle for anything less.

Made in the USA
Columbia, SC
06 January 2023

74183048R00121